Me
In Your
Longing

Failed In Love But Never Failed In Loving You.

MUDASIR MAGRY

For You My Dove (AR>>>28)

To The One Who Holds My Heart, This Book Is For You-A Journey Through My Thoughts And Memories, Reflecting The Beauty That Captivates Me Every Day. I Hope These Words Convey The Depth Of My Feelings And The Hope I Carry For Our Future Together

Contents

1. LIFE

" What Can I Say About Life,

Those People Who Used To Be Life Have Separated"

2. EVIL-DOER

"Love Is Evil-Doer!
Where Do You Flee Away?
Is There A Sorrow Troubling Your Day?

Why Do You Laugh So Freely, So Bright,
When Deep Down, There's A Shadow In Sight?

In This Vast World, We Often Go Unseen,
What Worth Do You Place On Your Own Being?

Your Turn Will Come; There's No Need To Fear,
Why Stand In Line When Your Time Is Near?

The Stone That Stands Firm Now, Was Once A Man Full Of
Life And Dreams,
This Is The Waiting That Love Often Seems."

3. SEPARATION

15

"The Pain Of Separation From You Is Greater Than Death!"

*"**My Dear Dove ,** In This Moment, I've Come To Understand That No Matter How Life Unfolds, I No Longer Seek Answers Or Explanations. The Pain Of Our Separation Has Taught Me The Power Of Forgiveness, And I Hold No Bitterness In My Heart.*

Though I Miss You Profoundly, This Distance Has Only Deepened My Love For You. You Are My Guiding Light, And Even In My Sorrow, My Feelings For You Remain Steadfast And True. I Cherish The Hope That We Will Soon Be Reunited, Where We Can Share Our Dreams And Joys Free From The Pain Of Parting."

4. HABIT

"In The Depths Of Our Shared Memories, I Find Myself Ensnared By The Habits We Formed Together. Every Time I Reach For My Phone, Your Number Instinctively Appears On The Screen, As If It's Etched In My Heart. It Feels Impossible To Escape The Pull Of Our Connection.

I've Made Countless Efforts To Move Away, To Create Space Between Us, But It's As If Every Part Of My World Remembers You. Even The Trees Outside Sway Gently, Echoing My Feelings, Longing For The Moments We Shared.

No Matter How Much I Try To Forget, The Bond We Created Lingers On, Reminding Me Of The Love That Still Exists Within Me. It's A Battle Between My Heart And My Mind, And I Wonder If There Will Ever Come A Day When I Can Truly Let Go.

But For Now, The Memories Of You Continue To Call Me Back, As Strong As Ever."

5. PATH

*"**My Dove,** Remember Those Paths We Travelled Together, Filled With Trust And Affection? They Were Beautiful, Vibrant, And Alive With The Essence Of Our Bond. Now, As I Walk This Journey Alone, It Feels Like A Punishment- A Heavy Weight On My Heart.*

You Were Once My Companion, The One Who Understood My Soul. But Now, In This New Chapter Of My Life, Everything Feels Different. It's As If My Heart Longs For The Past, Even While I Know You Are Irreplaceable.

Yet, Even In This Profound Love, I Sometimes Find Myself Longing For What We Shared, A Deep Yearning That Echoes Within Me. But Know This: My Love For You Is Unwavering, A Flame That Will Never Fade.

You Are My Past, My Present, And My Forever. I Cherish Every Moment We've Experienced Together, And I Hold You Close In My Heart. My Love For You Is All- Encompassing, And I Am Endlessly Grateful For The Bond We Share. You Are My Everything, And I Will Always Treasure You".

6. CHILDHOOD AND UNFULFILLED LONGINGS

"In This Vast Tapestry Of Our Lives, I Find Myself Longing For A Solace That Eludes Me-Your Heart, Where I Yearn To Find Refuge. Yet, Even As I Seek To Escape The Shadows Of This City That Binds Me, I Am Tethered To Its Memories Of You, Unable To Leave Behind The Essence Of What We Could Have Shared.

We Are Dreamers In A World Overflowing With Desires, Yet We Are Left With Our Unfulfilled Longings, Unable To Embrace The Love That Fate Intended For Us. Each Day, I Wander Through This Crowded Existence, Acutely Aware Of The Love That Remains Just Out Of Reach, A Silent Melody That Echoes In My Heart.

And In This Journey, I Realize That Youth Is Not Merely A Measure Of Age; It Is The Laughter And Mischief We Were Meant To Share. I Do Not Understand What It Means To Be Called Youthful. For Me, My Childhood Was Devoid Of The Carefree Mischief That Often Defines Those Early years.

I Remember A Time When The Laughter Of Friends Any They Thrill Of Adventure Seemed Like Distant Dreams, Overshadowed By Responsibilities And Burdens That Felt Far Too Heavy For Someone So Young.

While Others Revelled In Spontaneous Games And Innocent Pranks, I Often Found Myself Weighed Down By An Unshakeable Seriousness, Watching Life Unfold From The Side-lines. The Joy Of Carefree Play Seemed Like A

Privilege I Could Not Afford. Instead, I Grappled With A Sense Of Longing, Yearning For The Simplicity Of A World Where Joy Came Without Hesitation.

In This Reflection, I Feel The Deep Ache Of Lost Moments-Those Fleeting Chances To Be Wild And Free. The Essence Of Youth, So Often Romanticized, Seemed A Distant Echo In My Life. It's As If I Missed The Train To A Destination Filled With Laughter And Discovery, Left To Navigate A Landscape Shaped By Caution And Restraint.

In That Absence, I Learned To Appreciate The Quieter Moments, But I Also Carry The Weight Of What Could Have Been, A Shadow That Lingers Long After The Innocence Of Childhood Has Faded.

As I Pen These Words, I Want You To Know That Every Sentiment Is Woven With The Threads Of My Unspoken Love For You. I Cherish The Moments We've Yet To Experience And Hold Onto The Hope That One Day, We May Truly Share The Love That Has Lingered In The Silence Between Us".

7. YOUR PICTURE

"Keeping Your Picture Alongside Mine,

I've Spent This Lifetime With Great Care

With My Picture Beside Yours, I've Lived Each Day,

Building Memories Together In Every Way.

Every Moment With You Brings Me Joy And Peace,

In This Journey Of Love, My Happiness Won't Cease."

8. FATE

"In Every Glance, I See The Beauty Of Our Connection, Cherishing The Memories We've Created Together. Each Moment Feels Precious, As If Time Itself Has Slowed Down For Us.

This Story Has Been Buried With Me, Now Where Does Justice Stand With Chains? Our Love, Once Vibrant, Now Feels Like An Untold Tale Lost To The Ages. It Seems Like A Beautiful Dream Wrapped In Sorrow, Where Justice And Fairness Seem Far Away, Constrained By Circumstances We Cannot Control.

The One I Try To Make My Own Keeps Departing, My Fate Doesn't Allow Our Paths To Unite. Each Time I Reach Out, It Feels Like The Universe Pulls Us Apart. No Matter How Hard I Try To Bring You Closer, Fate Seems To Weave A Different Narrative For Us, One Filled With Separation And Longing.

But Despite This, My Heart Remains Steadfast. I Believe That Love Is Stronger Than Any Challenge We Face. I Hold Onto The Hope That One Day, Our Journeys Will Converge, And We 'll Find The Happiness We Both Deserve. Until Then, I'll Carry You In My Heart, Always Dreaming Of The Moment When Our Love Can Finally Flourish".

9. ALL OF YOU

*"**My Dearest Dove,** Without You, This World Feels Profoundly Empty. Every Moment Stretches Into Eternity, Reminding Me Of Your Absence. Please, Don't Say That Loyalty Holds No Value; It's What I Cherish Most. If You Were To Ask Me, I Would Commit To You Endlessly, For In This Bond, Without You, There Is Only Pain, No Joy To Be Found. I Cannot Settle For Anything Less Than Your Warmth And Affection.*

I Either Want All Of You-Your Laughter, Your Kindness, Your Spirit-Or I Want Nothing At All, I Find Myself Lost In An Ache That Words Cannot Describe. How Can I Know Where I'm Heading Or Why I Wander Through Life? Each Step I Take Feels Aimless, Like A Ship Without A Sail, Because Without You By My Side, I Feel Adrift And Incomplete.

Now, I Find It Hard Even To Hold Onto The Memories We Created, Accepting The Truth That Without You, Those Moments Feel Hollow. I've Tried To Distance Myself From The World, To Find Some Clarity.

Yet This Loneliness Is Heavy, A Weight I Cannot Bear Alone. The Silence Echoes In My Heart, And It Whispers Your Name, A Constant Reminder Of What We Shared And What I've Lost.

Every Day Apart Intensifies My Longing For You. I Realize How Deeply I Miss Your Smile, Your Voice, The Way You See Me. You Are The Missing Piece In My Life's Puzzle, The Light In My Darkness, The Only One Who Can Fill This Void That Grows With Each Passing Hour. Without You, Life Feels Like A Beautiful Song Without A Melody, And I Can't Help But Wish For The Day When We Can Create Our Symphony Again.

I Hope You Can Feel My Heart Reaching Out To You, How I Yearn For You To Return And Bring Joy Back Into My Life.

Together, We Can Mend The Fractures, Heal The Wounds Of The Past, For You Are Irreplaceable, My Love, The Very Essence Of My Soul's Desire. With You, I Believe I Can Be Whole Again, And Together, We Can Navigate This Journey With Hope And Love Anew. Embracing The Beauty Of Life, Cherishing You And Celebrating Our Love, Which Means Everything To Me".

10. PIECES

"When Someone Comes To Shatter My Heart, I Wish It To Be So Profound That It Leaves Everyone Who Witnesses It In Awe, Just Like The Way You Captured My Heart. Every Moment Without You Feels Like A Reminder Of The Pieces Of Myself That I'm Desperately Trying To Gather. I Often Wonder How Long I Can Keep Collecting These Fragments, All For The Hope Of Rekindling Our Connection.

Yet, I Ask Myself: How Long Can I Continue This Struggle? For You, I Would Endure Anything, But It's Challenging To Piece Myself Together When You're Not Here. The Weight Of Your Absence Feels Almost Unbearable.

In Your Absence, I Fear That Every Shard Of My Heart Might Prick Your Eyes, Reminding You Of What Once Was. I Wish For My Dreams Of Us To Stay Distant, Away From The Pain Of Reality. I Hope That No Part Of My Broken Heart Causes You Pain. I Want The Mirror Of My Dreams To Reflect Only Happiness, Far Away From The Sadness Of Our Reality.

I Wish For You To Feel No Pain From My Sorrow. I Want My Dreams To Remain Untouched By The Sadness Of Reality, A Sanctuary Where We Can Still Exist Together. It Pains Me To Think That Memories Might Hurt You, Even Inadvertently.

I Long For A Time When We Can Both Look Back And Smile, Free From Sorrow. I Find Myself Trying To Think Of Others, Only To Realize That No One Can Fill The Void You've Left. When I Glance At Anyone Else, It's As If The Intoxicating Essence Of Our Love Fades, Leaving Behind An Emptiness. Even Those Who Sit By My Side Remain Oblivious To My Struggles. They Don't See How I Break Over The Smallest Reminders Of You, How Trivial Matters Can Unravel Me.

I Wish I Could Heal Quickly, But Every Day Feels Like An Eternity Since My Dreams Of Us Have Shattered. Please Know That You Are Always In My Thoughts, And I Hold Onto The Hope That One Day We Will Find Our Way Back To Each Other".

11. VOWS

"Still, Memories Of The Past Come To Me From Time To Time,

The Pain Of Time Hasn't Really Diminished,

Wounds May Heal, But Scars Always Remain,

Distances Can't Erase Memories; They Linger On.

It's Also Possible That One Day, In Regret,

You May Come To Me, Steering Clear Of The World,

You, Who Are Innocent Yet Quick To Forget,

Even Embrace This Contradiction Of Yourself.

And I, Who Once Regarded You As My Saviour,

Would Bear Yet Another Wound As Before,

Standing Quietly On The Same Path Where Once Vows Were Broken"

12. SAVIOUR

"There Are Moments When I Find Myself Drifting Back To Our Shared Past, Feeling The Weight Of Memories That Still Hold Their Significance. Though Time Marches On, The Echoes Of Our Laughter And Whispers Linger Like Shadows. The Pain We Felt May Have Softened Over Time, But It's True: Scars Remain, Each One Telling A Story Of What We Once Shared.

I Think Of The Distance That Has Grown Between Us. It Reminds Me That Memories Are Resilient; They Thrive Despite The Space That May Separate Us. Sometimes, I Wonder If One Day You Might Find Your Way Back To Me, Perhaps Feeling A Pang Of Regret. Would You Choose To Escape The Noise Of The World, Seeking Solace In What We Once Had?

You, With Your Gentle Spirit, Sometimes So Quick To Forget, I Hope You Learn To Accept The Complexities Within Yourself. Embracing Your Innocence Alongside Your Moments Of Forgetfulness Is Part Of Your Beauty.

As For Me, I Remember The Way I Once Looked Up To You, Seeing In You A Kind Of Saviour. If Fate Were To Grant Me Another Wound, I Would Accept It Willingly, Standing On The Same Path Where Our Promises Once Thrived. Even If Those Promises Faded, The Love Behind Them Remains Unbroken In My Heart.

In This Reflection, I Wish For Us To Reconnect, Not Just With The Past, But With A Hope For The Future. Perhaps We Can Share Our Stories, Heal Together, And Redefine What We Mean To Each Other. No Matter What Has Happened, You Will Always Hold A Special Place In My Heart".

13. CIRCUMSTANCES

*"The Circumstances Of My Heart Have Shaped My
Current State;
In My Longing, I Lost Not Just The Desire, But My Entire
Essence.*

*Even After You Left, A Strange Atmosphere Lingered,
Your Memory Stayed Here, And Then Even That Faded
Away.*

*Your Hopes For Me Were Simple: Spend Your Life For A
Moment With You.
I Gave My Time Away For A Fleeting Connection, For A
Moment Of Brilliance.*

*My Heart Was Already Troubled, And Now It's Even
Worse;
What Was Your Absence, If Not A Delightful Pain For Me?*

*In Your Separation, I Indulged In The Essence Of Smoke,
Trying To Forget The Sweetness Of Your Presence.*

*I Had To Leave Your Street To Return To My Home,
It Was Just A Lane, Yet It's Shadow Now Stretches
Everywhere".*

14. ONE SORROW

"There Is One Sorrow That Will Never Leave My Heart, Why Didn't I Die Seeing You With Someone Else?"

*"**My Love,** There's A Deep Ache Within Me That Time Cannot Heal. It Lingers, A Shadow Over My Heart, Reminding Me Of Moments That Can Never Be Forgotten.*

When I Witness You With Someone Else, It Cuts Deeper Than Any Pain I've Known. In That Moment, I Question Why I'm Still Here, Alive To Feel This Torment.

Every Glance You Share, Every Laugh You Exchange, It Pulls At The Very Fabric Of My Being. I Wish I Could Escape This Heartache, But The Truth Is, It Binds Me To You.It Is A Reminder Of What We Could Have Had, The Love That Remains Unfulfilled.

Yet, In My Suffering, There's Also A Profound Admiration For The Joy You Bring To Others, Even If It Tears Me Apart.

So Here I Stand, Caught Between Love And Loss, Cherishing The Moments We've Shared While Grappling With The Sorrow Of What Might Never Be. You Are The Beautiful Dream I Can't Let Go Of, Even If It Means Living With This Heartache Forever". (one sorrow)

15. PEACEFUL LIFE

"Only This Trouble Lies In Forgetting You,

In Your Place, Who Should I Remember Instead?

Pretending To Be Happy Weighs On My Heart;

I Just Want To Find Real Joy.

Congratulations On Your Love's Richness;

I Just Wish For A Peaceful Life".

16. GHALIB

"In Reflecting On The Words Of Ghalib (Poet), I Find Truth That Resonates Deeply Within My Heart. He Spoke Of The Journey We All Undertake, Where With Each Passing Day, Even Our Sorrows Can Transform Into Something Healing.

As We Navigate The Complexities Of Life, Our Experiences —Both Joyful And Painful —Shape Us. Each Challenge We Face Together Strengthens Our Bond, Revealing Layers Of Love We Never Knew Existed.

It's In The Moments Of Struggle That We Find The Essence Of Our Connection; The Trials We Endure Become The Very Fabric Of Our Shared Story. Just As Ghalib Suggested, With Time, What Once Felt Like Unbearable Pain Can Lead To Growth And Understanding.

I Cherish Every Moment We Spend Together, Knowing That Even In Our Toughest Times, We Emerge Stronger And More United. You Are My Comfort And My Cure. Together, Let Us Embrace This Beautiful Journey, Where Love Transforms Our Hardships Into Strength And Tenderness".

17. YOUR LOVE

"In This Vast World, I Know That If I Search, I Might Stumble Upon Someone New. Yet, No Matter How Many Faces I Encounter, I Realize That No One Could Ever Love Me With The Depth And Intensity That You Do.

Your Love Is Unique, A Rare Gem That Lights Up My Life. I Can Imagine Someone Admiring Your Beauty, Captivated By Your Grace. But Even As They Gaze Upon you, They Will Never Possess The Understanding, The Shared Glances, Or The Unspoken Connection We Have.

Our Eyes Tell Stories Only We Can Comprehend, A Language That No One Else Can Interpret. It's Not Just Your Outer Beauty; It's The Way You See Me, The Way You Embrace My Flaws And Cherish My Dreams.

You Are My Heart's Desire, And Even In A Crowd, It's You I Seek. No One Else Can Fill The Space You Occupy In My Life"

18. JOURNEY

This Is How I Motivate Myself Now;

"Step Forward, My Companion, For We Must Walk And Also Burn.
Through The Long Days Of This Life, We Must Glow And Fade."

"As We Embark On This Journey Together, I Urge You To Take My Hand And Step Forward With Me. Life Is A Beautiful Path Filled With Moments Of Joy And Challenges Alike. We Must Walk Side By Side, Facing Each New Day With Courage And Passion.

Together, We Will Illuminate The Long Hours Of Our Lives. We Will Create Memories That Shimmer Like Stars, Even As We Navigate The Inevitable Shadows. Our Love Will Be Our Guiding Light, Allowing Us To Embrace Both The Warmth And The Trials That Come Our Way.

Let's Cherish Each Moment, Knowing That As We Burn Brightly With Love, We Will Also Gracefully Transition Through Life's Phases. With You By My Side, I Feel Ready To Face Whatever Lies Ahead —Together, We Will Shine And Gracefully Let Go As The Days Unfold".

19. USED TO

"Let's Not Fall In Love; We're Used To It.

So What Should We Do? We've Grown Accustomed To Each Other.

Don't Waste Your Skill Of The Hourglass;

I Am A Mirror, And I'm Used To Breaking.

What Can I Say? Why Can't I Be Patient?

What Can I Do? I'm Used To Seeing You.

In union, The Distances Remain Just Like In Separation,

For You, Sleep Is A Habit, while I Stay Awake At Night.

How Long Will This Torment Last?

For Someone Who Has The Habit Of Forgetting,

Don't Remember Those Who Have Learned To Forget."

20. FROM ABOVE

"When I Look From The Sky,

I See The Vast Expanse Of Land Below.

In This Great Expanse, There Lies A Small City,

Within This Small City, A Web Of Streets Unfolds.

Among These Streets, Hidden Away

Is A Desolate Lane, Lonely And Quiet.

At The Turn Of This Lonely Lane Stands A Solitary Tree,

Beneath Its Shade, A Humble Little House Waits.

Inside This Small House, A Garden Of Untamed Earth,

Where A Blooming Rose Unfolds Its Petals.

In The Fragrance Of That Rose,

There's The Scent Of My Beloved's Skin.

Within That Fragrant Presence Lies A Heart,

A Heart That Beats Like An Ocean, Deep And Vast.

In The Expanse Of That Heart, I Seem To Have Lost Myself,

As If I've Grown Larger Than This World Around Me."

22. BY HEART

"I Remember The Hues Of The Evening And Those Beautiful Nights,

Where All Realities Fade Away, Leaving Only A Cherished Story In My Heart.

With Tears, I Paint Your Image, A Masterpiece Made From My Emotions,

For In My Eyes, Your Face Lingers, Speaking To Me In A Language Only We Understand".

23. SMILED

"As I Wander Through The Corridors Of My Memories, I Realize How Deeply I've Forgotten Everything But You. Is It Really You I See Before Me? It Feels Surreal, As If The Past Has Faded Away, Leaving Me In A Haze.

In A World Where Connections Often Lose Their Meaning, I Wonder What It Even Means To Uphold Those Bonds We Once Held Dear. We Smiled When We Met, If Only Joy Hadn't Turned To Tears.

The Love We Shared Seems Like A Distant Echo Now, With Memories Fading Into Shadows. Why Has The Vibrancy Of Our Affection Vanished From My Heart? My Soul Feels Empty Without The Passion We Once Ignited.

Yet, Even In Moments When Our Paths Cross, I Wonder If That Spark Still Lingers. Do We Still Hold The Essence Of What We Once Were? My Heart Longs For The Warmth Of Your Presence, Hoping To Revive The Colours Of Our Love".

23. SOMEONE LIKE YOU

"When I Gaze At Someone Like You,

It's Not Just The Mere Mention Of My Name That Matters.

Your Presence Fills My Thoughts,

Yet You Remain Blissfully Unaware Of The Depths I Feel.

What Do You Know Of The Longing In My Heart?

How Deeply Have You Connected With My Soul?

It's As If Time Stood Still,

And After What Felt Like An Eternity, Our Hands Finally Touched.

With Each Brush Of Your Skin, My Heart Raced,

As If We'd Finally Reached The Shore Of Our Shared Dreams.

I Remember That Moment Vividly-In Front Of The World,
You Kissed Me,

A Declaration Of Our Love, And Suddenly, Our Story
Became A Tale For Everyone To Know.

The Whispers Of Our Romance Echoed,

As If The Universe Conspired To Witness Our Joy.

Each Glance, Each Touch, Each Shared Laugh,

Became A Thread Woven Into The Fabric Of Our Lives".

24. DRIED FLOWERS

"Now That We've Parted, Perhaps We'll Meet Again In Dreams,

Like Dried Flowers Found In Old Books.

Take The Sorrows Of This World And Blend Them With Our Love,

For The Intoxication Grows When We Find Solace Above.

Seek The Pearls Of Loyalty Among The Scattered Souls,

This Treasure Could Be Yours, Even In Shattered Roles.

You Are Not A God, Nor Is My Love Like Angels' Grace,

We Are But Humans; Why This Distance We Embrace?

Today We Were Drawn To The Same Thoughts And Fears,

How Strange That Tomorrow, They'll Echo Through The Years.

Neither You Are Here, Nor I, Nor Is The Past We Knew,
Like Two Beings Lost, Chasing Illusions Anew".

25. HANDFUL OF DUST

"I Am Not The Light Of Anyone's Eyes,

Nor The Comfort Of Anyone's Heart.

I Am The Handful Of Dust,

That Cannot Be Of Help To Anyone.

I Am Not The Remedy For Heartache,

Nor The Sweet Gaze Of Anyone.

I Am Neither Here Nor There,

Neither Solace Nor Disturbance.

My Colour And Form Have Faded,

Time Has Drifted Away From Me.

The Garden Has Withered Away,

I Am The Very Spring Of Someone's Hope.

I Long To Be Found, To Grow And To Start,

To Bring Back The Joy,

And Heal A Warm Heart".

26. TIDE OF TEARS

"I Seek Again Those Leisurely Nights And Days,

When I Could Sit Lost In Thoughts Of My Beloved.

Do Not Stir Us Again With The Tide Of Tears,

For We Sit Here, Poised Amidst The Storm Of Emotions".

27. HEART THINKS OF YOU

"Life Goes On Like This,

Without Any Longing For Someone's Support.

No Path, No Destination, No Trace Of Light,

My Life Wanders In Darkness,

I Know I Might Get Lost In These Shadows,

Yet Sometimes, My Heart Thinks Of You".

28. DESIRES

"In My Heart, Desire Has Slipped Away,

Those Deep Lashes Have Cast A Heavy Shadow,

I Longed To Draw My Portrait Within You,

And In Silence, I Tugged At Your Flowing Hair.

Every State Of My Reason And Sense,

You Forged In The Mould Of Your Wild Passion,

I Had Vowed To Turn Away From Love's Grasp,

Yet You Wrapped Me In Your Embrace Once More".

In Regret of Separation:

"In This Sorrow, I Find My Thoughts Drifting,

Sleep Begins To Embrace Me In This Absence,

Though I Have Reasons Against Your Love,

I Ponder In Defence Of Your Essence.

The Soul Has Whispered Sweet Deceptions Of Love,

While The Body Grapples With Its Disdain,

Now, Only Habits Occupy My Days,

My Spirit Not Entwined In Complaints Or Pain.

Do Not Bring Love Into Our Midst,

I Scream, Overwhelmed By The Effects It Leaves,

It's Not So Simple For Me To Endure,

We Still Hold On To Our Little Deceits.

What Was To Be Built Now Lies In Flames,

The Fire Consumed That Hopeful Space,

How To Articulate This Longing Of Mine,

When Venom Has Seeped Into This Place.

In The Void, I Contemplate Alone,

What Conversation Can Arise In Silence?

How Will Life Unfold In This Desolation?

My Heart Refuses To Find Solace In Love".

29. SIDE BY SIDE

"I Walk Close To You, Side By Side,

Each Step A Dance Where Our Souls Collide.

I Drift Like A Breeze, Just As You Do,

In The Rhythm Of Life, It's Always With You.

You Are The Heart Of Every Gathering,

No Longer Do I Shy From The World's Wandering.

What Words Can Express What My Heart Knows?

With Those Who Are Joyful, My Spirit Flows.

A Journey Awaits, Distant Yet Near,

Sometimes We Stumble, But Still Persevere.

In The Twilight Of Choices, A Crossroads We Face,

If We Falter, Our Hearts Still Embrace.

I Wonder How I'm Unravelling Slowly,

While Onlookers Watch, Their Gazes So Lonely.

You Become The Colour, The Fragrance, The Light,

In Every Verse, I Find You, So Bright.

With Every Whisper And Touch Of Your Hand,

I Surrender My Thoughts To This Love We've Planned.

Let The World Around Us Fade Into Mist,

For In Your Presence, There's Nothing Amiss".

30. WOUNDS OF LONGING

"Our Wounds Of Longing Have Grown Old,

For We've Travelled Down That Lane Where Memories Unfold.

You Should Not Heed The Whispers Of Those Who Adore You,

For Your Admirers Have Become Reckless In Their Pursuit.

When Those Tresses Recall Our Bittersweet Separation,

Clouds Gather, Turning Into A Gentle Celebration.

The Times We Shared, Unique In Their Own Way,

Have Turned Into Stories That Linger In The Day.

Today, A Fragrant Essence Wafted From Your Abode,

Where Nightingales Now Find Their Cherished Road.

May Those Who Come After Us Be Blessed And Free,

For The Place We Once Knew Has Transformed Beautifully.

Each Moment With You Was Like A Tender Dawn,

Now, Echoes Of Our Laughter Continue On And On.

In Your Presence, I Discovered A World So Divine,

A Sanctuary Built On Love, Eternally Intertwined.

Let Us Treasure The Dreams We've Woven In Time,

For Even As Seasons Change, Our Love Will Forever Rhyme.

So Here's To Us, To The Memories Yet To Unfold,

In A Tapestry Of Love, Let Our Hearts Be Bold".

31. FALLING APART

*"Every Time You Come Before Me,
I Find Myself Falling Apart,*

*Each Encounter Leaves Me More Distant,
As If You're A Puzzle, Yet Uncharted,*

*Who Are You? You Don't Know Your Heart.
Who Am I? A Stranger In My Own Heart.*

*You Claim To Know Me, Yet You Hold Me In Chains,
With A Passion That Feels Both Like Curse And Grace.*

*You Stand On The Ground Where I Do Not Reign,
And I Am But A Whisper In This Infinite Space.*

*I've Wandered Through Love, A Novice In Despair,
While You Embody The Height Of What Love Can Be.*

*Never Did I Declare That Love Brings Release,
Nor Promised Loyalty When Shadows Fall.*

*So, Pour Your Treasures Over My Weary Soul,
But Know This: In The Market Of Love, You Must Remain
Pure.*

When I Cannot Give You The Joy That Love Deserves,
And In My Sorrows, I Fail To Offer Solace,

You Hold No Claim To Tear Me Apart.
For All My Dreams Are Caught In The Winds Of Betrayal,
Each Flickering Light A Reminder Of Pain,

So, You Must Not Seek To Claim Me,
Nor Should You Take Away The Solitude I've Gained.

In This Intricate Dance Of Love And Despair,
Let's Acknowledge The Distance That Binds Us Still,

For While My Heart Yearns For Your Radiant Care,
I Must Protect It From A Love That Cannot Fulfil".

32. BEAUTIFUL SOUL

"I Keep Remembering That Beautiful Soul,
In This Endless Fire, I Burn Day And Night.

Oh, When Will You See Me With Those Enchanting Eyes?
I Wander Through Your Street, Longing For Your Gaze.

I Love Deeply, Not Driven By Mere Desire,
That's Why I Find Myself Lost In Every Thought Of You.

No One Should Suspect That I Shed Tears,
So I Wear A Smile While Hiding My Sorrows.

Otherwise, For A Long Time, I Would Have Left This World Behind,
It's Your Pain That Keeps Me Alive, Gives Me Breath.

Each Fragment Of Your Sorrow, I Cradle Close,
Turning My Heart Into A Sanctuary For Your Grief".

33. THOUSAND TIMES

"A Thousand Times I've Said…
That My Love Is For You,
Yet It Seems My Words,
Leave No Mark On You.
Then What Should I Do.

When My Heart Cries Out,
In The Silence Between Us,
What's This Love About?

Every Glance, Every Touch,
Holds A Universe Inside,
But If You Don't Feel It,
Where Does My Longing Hide?

I Pour My Soul Into The Night,
Whisper Your Name In The Stars,
Yet It Feels Like I'm Calling
To The Silence, To The Scars.

Is There A Way To Bridge This Space,
To Make You See, To Make You Feel?
For Every Heartbeat, Every Sigh,
Is A Promise, A Dream So Real.

So I'll Keep Saying It,
A Thousand Times More,
For Love Like This,
Is Worth Fighting For.

Through Every Doubt, Every Fear,
I'll Stand By You, Steadfast And True,
Because My Heart Knows One Truth-
I Am Endlessly In Love With You".

34. HEART'S FAVOURITE

"In The Quiet Moments, When The World Seemed Vast,

We Found Ourselves Lost In The Beauty Of The Past.

Over The Simplest Things, We Used To Blush,

In The Depths Of Our Hearts, There Was Always A Hush.

We Crafted Our Words With Care, Each Phrase A Dance,

In The Delicate Silence, We Nurtured Our Chance.

But Now, As I Stand, Perhaps It Feels Distant,

Yet The Truth Remains-My Love For You Is Persistent.

Though It May Not Seem So Now,

But Know That Once Upon A Time I Was Your Heart's Favourite.

In Every Stolen Glance And Every Shy Smile,

I Was Yours, My Love, Across Every Mile".

35. LOVE'S MADNESS

"In Love's Madness, No One's Quite Like Me,

But Still, I Hold My Heart, Tenderly Free.

Yet I Find Myself, Caught In This Dance,

A Piece Of My Soul, Lost In Your Glance.

You Are My Echo, My Breath, My Song,

In A World Where I've Felt I Never Belonged.

Each Heartbeat Whispers Your Name In The Night,

A Soft, Gentle Promise, A Guiding Light.

I'm More Than A Shadow, More Than A Dream,

With Every Glance, I Feel The Gleam.

But I'm Just A Fraction, A Whisper, A Sigh,

A Fraction Of Love, Beneath The Vast Sky.

If Only You Knew The Depths Of My Heart,

How Every Moment We Share Is A Work Of Art.

With You, I Am Whole, Yet Still Feel So Small,

In The Grand Tapestry Of Love, You're My All.

So Here's My Confession, Laid Bare And True,

In This Beautiful Madness, My Heart Beats For You.

No More Than A Fragment, Yet Infinite Still,

For You Are My Love, My Passion, My Will".

36. YOUR TOUCH

*"As You Leave, Touch Some Things In This Room,
I'll Cherish How Your Hands Felt Against Them.*

*Yet, I Mourn The Fact That I Haven't Conquered Your
Eyes,
What A Futile Time To Be Born, Trapped In Unfulfilled
Desire.*

*When You Turn To Leave, The Air Grows Heavy,
Each Corner Echoes With Your Laughter And Light.*

*In This Stillness, I Feel The Weight Of My Longing,
A Haunting Reminder Of A Love I've Yet To Claim.*

*Even As You Walk Away, I'll hold You Close, In Every
Memory, Your Essence Lingers On.*

*A Bond So Profound, It Defies The Passage Of Time,
In This World Where Precious Moments Slip Away Too
Swiftly".*

37. PATHS OF LIFE

"As We Wander Through The Paths Of Life,

In Solitude's Embrace, We Strive And Fight.

What Else Have I Done, In This Endless Chase,

But Made Each Day A Journey, Our Hearts Alight.

Through The Quiet Whispers Of Night's Gentle Breeze,

I Search For Your Presence In Every Rustle Of Leaves.

Each Moment Apart Feels Like A Thousand Years,

Yet In Dreams, Your Laughter Dances, And My Heart Believes.

I've Wandered These Roads, Both Winding And Bare,

With Your Memories Guiding Me, Soft As A Prayer.

In Every Shadow And Every Dawn's Glow,

It's Your Love That I Cherish, The Light I Follow.

In This Vast World, Where We Sometimes Lose Our Way,

Your Essence Lingers In The Words I Say.

Though Life May Test Us, And Time May Confine,

My Heart Knows A Truth: Forever You're Mine.

So Let Us Embrace Each Step That We Take,

In This Beautiful Dance, For Love's Own Sake.

Together We'll Conquer, Together We'll Stand,

Hand In Hand, Forever, In This Promised Land".

38. WHEN YOU COME

*"When You Come, You Will Find Me Lost In The Echoes Of
Your Absence,
In This Silence That Stretches Beyond The Confines Of
Dreams.*

*Is It Your Wish To Fill This Empty Room With Your
Laughter?
Yet Here, Amidst The Whispers Of Books, I Dwell Alone.*

*Each Page, A Reminder Of What Could Have Been,
These Stories Speak Of Love And Loss,
Yet Leave Me Yearning For Your Presence.
They've Crafted A Prison Of Longing,
A Cruel Twist In The Tale Of My Heart.*

*Within These Volumes Lies A Hidden Truth,
A Secret My Restless Mind Desperately Seeks To Unveil.*

*A Promise Of Joy That Eludes My Grasp,
For Without You, Life Feels Like A Book Without An
Ending,
A Melody Without A Note,
A Soul Forever In Search Of Solace.*

So, My Love, When You Finally Arrive,
You Will Breathe Life Into This Desolate Space.
You Will Transform My Solitude Into A Symphony,

Turning Each Silent Moment Into A Cherished Memory.
Together, We Will Rewrite This Narrative,
Where Joy Finds Its Resolution,
And The Warmth Of Your Embrace Brings Peace To My
Weary Heart.

In Your Presence, The Walls Will No Longer Echo With
Solitude,
But Will Instead Resonate With The Sweet Cadence Of
Love".

Sometimes My Mind To My Heart;
"My Dove, Why Must We Forge A New Connection,
When We Both Know That Time Might Pull Us Apart?

If Destiny Demands Separation, Let's Not Squabble,
Why Not Let The Silence Speak Volumes In Our Hearts?

It's Enough That We Share No Animosity;
What's The Use Of Declaring Loyalty In A Fleeting
Moment?

Those Beautiful Words-faithfulness, Sincerity, Sacrifice,
Love-
Why Pursue Them When Our Hearts Seem To Drift?

Remember The Promises We Exchanged In Whispers,
Why Should We Bear The Weight Of Those Moments
Forever?

Why Must Our Dreams Always Intertwine,
When Your Soul's Wishes Shine Brightly On Their Own?

Let Us Not Be Burdened By Unspoken Expectations,
Why Confine Our Love To The Walls Of Doubt And Fear?

If Our Hearts Crave The Freedom Of The World,
Why Not Embrace The Sunlight Rather Than Linger In
Shadows?

We Are Both Part Of This Vast Universe,
So Let's Believe In Our Own Strength And Essence.

When The World Turns A Blind Eye To Our Existence,
Why Should We Let Its Indifference Haunt Our Hearts?

In The End, My Dear, It Is Enough For Me
That Our Paths Crossed, Even If They Diverge.

Let's Cherish The Moments We Had,
And Find Peace In The Love We Shared,

For Even In Separation, Your Essence Remains,
A Beautiful Memory Etched In My Soul Forever".

39. HEARTLESSNESS

*"Let Days Pass By In This Silent Surrender,
As Long As We Breathe, We Teeter On The Edge Of
Oblivion.*

*Thoughts Wander Like Lost Souls In The Night,
While The World Awakens, Blind To Our Aching Hearts.*

*Oh, How You Captivate Me, Like The First Light Of Dawn,
And Yet, In Your Presence, I Feel A Profound Loneliness.*

*It's A Cruel Fate That Whispers We Might Fade Away,
Like Fleeting Shadows, Swallowed By The Dark.*

*Shyness Cloaks You, A Fragile Shroud,
Fear Wraps Around Us Like A Heavy Chain. Why Do You
Hesitate To Unveil Your Heart?
You! Yes, You! But Why Won't You Say My Name?*

*In This Dance Of Unspoken Desires,
I Long For The Courage To Shatter This Silence.*

*To Hold Your Gaze And Drown In Your Depths,
To Share Dreams And Weave A tapestry Of Us.*

Let's Defy This Transient Existence,
Embrace The Fleeting Magic In Every Heartbeat.

For If We Must Face The End, Let It Be Together,
With Our Souls Entwined, Our Names Forever Whispered
In The Wind.

Every Moment Without You Is A Wound,
A Reminder That Love's Light Is Often Dimmed.

So, Let Us Carve Our Names Into The Stars,
And Create A Universe Where Our Love Can Thrive,
Unbound.

In The Quiet Of The Night, When The World Sleeps,
I'll Wait For You, My Heart Aching To Be known.

For In Your Eyes, I See A Thousand Lifetimes,
And In Your Silence, I Feel The Weight Of Forever".

40. ASHAMED

"I Am Very Ashamed Of My Existence, For I Met You,
While You Were Full of Joy And Happiness, Yet Received
Only Sorrow.

I Don't Grieve For Not Finding Myself Within,
The Sorrow Lies In The Fact That You Too Found Little Of
Yourself,

In The Balance Of My Heart, A Reckoning Unfolds,
I Blush At The Thought Of What I Never Told,

What Did You Find In Your World Of Desire And Longing?
Even When We Met, You Found Only Chaos And Turmoil,

In My Heart, Only Fragments Of Longing Conspired.
Now, In Your Own Way, You've Drifted Afar,
Wishing You Could Find Yourself, A Guiding Star,

In This City Of Tumult, I Found A Secret Friend,
But To You, My Love, I Wish The Same To Send.

I Pray For The Joy Of Your Laughter To Return,
May Your Heart Be Filled With The Warmth You Yearn,

ME IN YOUR LONGING

Though I Have Never Truly Grasped Your Soul,
I Hope You Find The Peace That Makes You Whole.

You Journeyed Through My Heart For Many Days, Left
Footprints In Time,
I'm Left With The Echoes Of A Love So Sublime,

If Only Another Could Sweep You Off Your Feet,
If Only I Could Be The One To Make You Complete.

Yet, Here I Stand, With Memories That Bind,
A Love Unyielding, A Connection Defined,

Even Apart, My Heart Continues To Ache,
For The Moments We Shared, For The Risks I would Take.

So Here's My Wish, My Silent Prayer,
That You Find Joy And Love Everywhere,

Though Paths Diverge, My Feelings Remain,
In Every Heartbeat, I Call Out Your Name".

41. SUNSET

"My Love, Every Sunset Reminds Me Of You, The Way The Colours Blend In The Sky Mirrors The Way Your Presence Colours My Life. In Those Serene Moments, I Find Solace, As If The World Around Us Fades, Leaving Just The Two Of Us In A Timeless Embrace.

Each Tear I Shed Is A Brushstrokes On The Canvas Of My Memories, Where Your Laughter Echoes And Your Smile Shines Brightly. You Are More Than Just A Memory; You Are My Muse, My Inspiration, The Very Essence Of My Dreams.

As I Close My Eyes, I Can See You Clearly, Your Face Illuminated By The Soft Glow Of The Evening. It's As If The Universe Conspired To Bring Your Beauty To Life In My Mind, Speaking To Me In Whispers Of Love And Longing.

Every Moment Spent With You Is Etched In My Heart, A Story That Grows Richer With Each Passing Day. I Cherish Our Time Together, Knowing That Even In The Silence, Our Souls Communicate In Ways Words Cannot Express. Forever, I will Hold Onto These Memories, For They Are A Testament To The Love We Share-A Love That Transcends The Ordinary, Making Every Moment Magical. You Are My Evening, My Night, My Everything"

42. LOVE

"Love Is The Essence Of Life,
Without It, Life Loses Its Flavour.

May I Have Permission To Speak?
Though, Perhaps, There's Nothing To Say.

When At Last, After Many Years, I See You,
What Will There Be But Formalities Between Us?

Until Our Passions Flourish Anew,
Your Charm And Beauty Will Have Already Captivated
Another.

I've Heard Whispers Of An Unfolding Tale,
That Perhaps, Like A Wandering Soul, You Have Been Left
Behind".

43. GARDENER

How Cruel Are Those Who Say,

"Break The Flowers, Don't Pluck Them."

We Are The Gardeners Of This Thought,

"Look At The Flowers, Don't Break Them."

But In Your Presence, My Heart Blooms,

A Garden Flourishing In Your Light.

Each Petal Whispers Secrets Of Love,

Fragile Yet Fierce, They Hold Our Dreams.

We Are The Caretakers Of This Moment,

Preserving Beauty, Cherishing Each Glance.

In A World That Rushes To Destroy,

I Find Solace In Your Gentle Spirit.

Together, Let's Nurture This Garden,

Where Love Blossoms Without Fear.

So Let Us Wander Through This Paradise,

Where Every Flower Tells Our Story.

For In Your Eyes, I See The Essence,

Of A Love That Blooms Eternally,

A Bond Too Precious To Ever Break".

44. UNCERTAINTIES

"As I Sit Here Thinking Of You, It Strikes Me How Profound The Idea Is That Now That We've Parted, Perhaps We'll Meet Again In Our Dreams, Just Like Dried Flowers Nestled In The Pages Of Old Books. Those Memories We Created Together Hold A beauty That Time Cannot Erase.

In This World Filled With Its Challenges, I Often Find Solace In The Thought Of Blending Our Joys And Sorrows. It's As If Our Love Has The Power To Transform Even The Darkest Moments Into Something Meaningful.

I Want You To Know That I Carry You With Me Through Every Hardship, And Your Essence Makes Everything Feel Lighter.

I Believe We Can Find Loyalty And Sincerity Amid The Chaos Of Life. Like Hidden Treasures Waiting To Be Discovered, The Connection We Share Is Something Rare And Precious. Even When It Seems That The World Is Full Of Fleeting Encounters, What We Have Is Something Worth Holding Onto.

Sometimes, I Wonder Why We Allow Distance To Come Between Us. It Feels Strange That Two People, Who Share So Much, Can Be Separated By Invisible Barriers. As I Think About The Thoughts And Fears That Draw Us Together Today, I Realize How Deeply Intertwined Our Lives Are. Tomorrow May Bring Its Uncertainties, But The Memories We've Built Together Will Forever Echo In My Heart".

45. HOME

"Now Emerge From Within Yourself,
Come Forth From The Depths Of Your Being,
For This Home Needs Your Essence,

Once Vibrant, Now Feels Barren Without Your Light.
I've Come To Understand That What Is Lacking-Your
Laughter, Your Warmth, Is The True Beauty Of Life.

My Heart's Desires Have Drifted Away,
Left Me Alone To Wrestle With This Deep-Seated Pain.
People Pass By, Knowing Me Only As A Busy Soul,
Yet They Cannot See That My Sorrow Has Become My
Quiet Companion.

Today Unfolded Like Any Other,
Yet Every Moment Felt Heavy, Weighted By Your Absence.
From Head To Toe, My Body Still Stands,
But Without You, It's Merely A Shell-Lifeless And Hollow".

46. TIDES OF FATE

"Sometimes, As The Day Gives Way To Night,
I Sit In Quiet Reflection, Pondering Our Moments,
Wondering If What We Had Was Real Or Just A Dream.

You Brought Such Joy Into My Life,
A Joy That Lingered Like A Sweet Fragrance,
But Now, I Find Myself Lost In Thoughts-
Do You Think Of Me As I Think Of You?

Each Time You Cross My Mind,
I Feel That Familiar Ache Of Longing,
Like A Soft Whisper Of Hope That Refuses To Fade.

Is That Warmth Still There In Your Heart?
Or Has It Dimmed Like The Fading Light Of Day,
Leaving Shadows Where Our Love Once Danced?

You Were My Everything, My Reason To Breathe,
But Now I Wonder-Do You Still Hold A Piece Of Me?
In A World That Knows My Name Yet Forgets My Essence,

Do You Still See Me As I Once Was,
Or Have I Become Just A Fleeting Memory?

Love, They Say, Is Eternal-
Yet Here We Are, Standing At This Crossroads,
Possibly For The Last Time,
With The Weight Of Our Shared History Heavy Upon Us.

Have You Let Go Of The Moments We Cherished,
Lost In The Rush Of Life, While I Remain?

I Reach Out Through The Silence,
Hoping To Bridge The Gap That Time Has Created,
Desperate For A Sign That You Remember,
That The Love We Shared Still Echoes Somewhere Deep
Within.

So Tell Me, My Dear-Is There Still A Flicker Of What We
Were,
Or Has It All Been Washed Away By The Tides Of Fate?

47. ENDLESS

"Life Flows Around Me In A Way That Feels Endless And Unanchored, Devoid Of The Warmth That Comes From Being Close To Someone. Each Day Feels Like Wandering Through A Maze Of Shadows, Where I Find No Clear Path Or Light To Guide Me.

In This Vast Expanse Of Darkness, I Often Feel Like I'm Losing Myself. But Amidst This Gloom, There's A Flicker Of Hope That You Bring. Though I May Feel Lost, Thoughts Of You Light Up My Heart. You Are The Echo That Resonates Within Me, A Whisper That Reminds Me That There Is Beauty Even In Darkness.

Sometimes, When The World Feels Too Heavy, I Close My Eyes And Imagine You Beside Me. Your Smile, Your Laughter, They Pierce Through The Night Like Stars In A Cloudy Sky. It's In These Moments That I Realize How Deeply I Long For You, How Your Presence Could Illuminate The Darkest Corners Of My Life.

Though Life May Not Always Have A Clear Direction, I Know That With You, Every Step, Even In Uncertainty, Would Feel Like A Journey Worth Taking. You Are The Thought That Dances Through My Mind, The Dream I Cherish. I Hope To Find You, To Share This Journey Together, Turning Shadows Into Light, And Loneliness Into Companionship".

48. UNOPENED BOOK

"As I Pen These Words, I Am Reminded Of The Delicate Dance Between Longing And Revelation. I Implore You, Let Not The Glass Of Our Connection Remain Empty. Each Moment We Share Is A Celestial Moment, Much Like The Moon That Gently Bathes Our Gathering In Its Glow, Casting A Light On The Shadows Of Our Unspoken Feelings.

If Only The Vibrant Hues Of Spring Could Embrace Us, Igniting A Fire Within Our Hearts. If Only The Right Season Would Arrive-One That Would Allow Us To Openly Express The Fervour We Both Feel. There's A Beauty In The Fleeting Moments That We Steal From The World, A Beauty That Should Not Be Shrouded In Silence.

Your Absence Weighs Heavily Upon Me; It Feels As If I've Chronicled Our Love In Volumes Yet To Be Read. Despite This, My Heart Seems To Keep Its Secrets, Refusing To Open Up Fully To You.

I Often Found Myself Lost In The Belief That I Understood This Role We Play In Each Other's Lives-Yet, I Now See It As An Unfinished Story, Yearning For More Chapters Filled With Joy And Connection.

Perhaps Love Is A Teacher That Gently Guides Us Through The Complexities Of Our Emotions. It Shows Us That Sometimes, Even The Act Of Denial Can Stem From Deep Affection.

Yet Within Me, The Sacredness Of What We Have Feels Like An Unopened Book, Waiting For The Right Moment To Reveal Its Pages".

49. SILENT PRAYERS

"In The Quiet Of The Night, I Remember Our Dreams,
The Ones We Painted In Colours So Bright, Reaching For
The Stars,
Yet Here We Are, As If Those Dreams Have Wilted,
Now Resting Softly, Close To The Earth, Where Hope
Seems Far.

Once, We Vowed To Journey Together,
To Face The Storms, Hand In Hand, Till The Very End.
But As Time Weaves It's Intricate Tapestry,
I Find Our Talks Drifting To Silent Prayers Instead.

I Long For The Days When Our Laughter Echoed,
When Every Moment Felt Like Forever Intertwined.
Now, As Shadows Linger, I Search For A Spark,
A Glimmer Of The Love We Promised, So Kind.

Let Us Revive Those Dreams, My Love,
Reach Once More For The Heights We Envisioned.
For Every Wilted Petal, There's A Chance To Bloom
Anew,
Let Our Hearts Embrace The Magic Of Our Shared Vision.

*Though The Road May Seem Heavy, And Doubts May
Arise,
Together, We Can Chase The Light Beyond The Dark
Skies.
With Every Prayer, Let's Weave A New Promise,
To Cherish Our Love, Eternally Bound, Limitless.*

*So Here's My Heart, Laid Bare Before You,
Let's Reignite The Flames Of Our Beautiful Past.
For In Your Eyes, I See The Stars Once More,
And With You, My Love, I Know We'll Forever Last".*

50. PROFOUND CONNECTION

"In The Depths Of My Heart, You Dwell, A Beautiful Memory That Ignites A Fire Within Me. Each Day Is A Dance Between Joy And Longing, As I Navigate The Streets Where You Once Walked, Where Our Laughter Echoed Like A Sweet Melody. I Find Myself Caught In The Rhythm Of Your Essence, Aching To Catch A Glimpse Of You Through The World's Chaos.

My Love For You Transcends Mere Attraction; It Is A Profound Connection That Consumes Me Entirely. I Wear A Mask Of Laughter, But Beneath It Lies A River Of Emotions, Flowing Silently. I Refuse To Let The World See My Tears, For I Want To Be Your Strength, The Light In Your Darkness.

If Only You Could Understand The Weight Of My Devotion. Each Fragment Of Your Pain Is A Treasure I Hold Dear, For It Intertwines With My Very Being. You Are My Reason, My Inspiration. In The Quiet Moments When The World Fades Away, It Is Your Spirit That Brings Me Solace".

51. DRY RIVER

"I Haven't Seen You For Many Days,
Yet You Reside In The Deepest Corners Of My Heart.

Though The World Moves On, You Are My Constant
Thought,
An Unchanging Presence That Colours My Days.

How Did I First Catch A Glimpse Of You,
That Moment When My Heart Recognized Its Home?

Since Then, Time Has Stood Still;
I Find Myself Lost, Echoing Your Name In Silence.

The Dry River Reminds Me Of Our Moments,
A Once Vibrant Stream Now Barren Without Your
Laughter.

I Recall The Times We Shared,
Where Joy Flowed As Freely As Water,
Now I Wander Through Memories,
And I Haven't She'd A Tear In Many Days-
Not From Sorrow, But From The Longing
That Fills My Soul When You Are Far Away.

ME IN YOUR LONGING

Every Star In The Night Sky Whispers Your Name,
Each Breeze Carries The Scent Of Your Essence,
I Yearn For The Warmth Of Your Smile,
For The Soft Touch Of Your Hand In Mine.

Though We May Be Apart,
You Are Woven Into The Fabric Of My Being.

My Love, I Promise To Wait,
For The Day Our Paths Cross Once More,
And I Can Finally Tell You,
Just How Profoundly You Are Missed.

Until Then, I Carry You With Me,
In Every Heartbeat, In Every Sigh,
A Love That Knows No Distance,
A Connection That Time Cannot Sever".

52. STAR

"In Life, There Once Shone A Star,

So Precious, Yet Now So Far.

Though It Faded Into The Night,

Its Brilliance Still Holds My Heart Tight.

Look At The Sky, The Joy It Brings,

Countless Stars On Silent Wings.

How Many Love Stories Have Ended,

How Many Dreams, Sweetly Suspended?

Yet When We Ponder Those Fallen Lights,

Does The Sky Mourn For Its Lost Delights?

No, The Cosmos Continues To Dance,

Embracing The Fleeting, The Lost Romance.

ME IN YOUR LONGING

So What's past Is Past, Let It Be,

For Love's Memory Still Lives In Me.

Though Moments Fade, Their Essence Stays,

Guiding My Heart Through Life's Tangled Maze.

With Every Star That Flickers And Fades,

I Cherish The Love That Never Evades.

For In Every Loss, A Lesson Unfolds,

In The Stories Of Lovers, Their Glories Retold.

So Here I Stand, With Heart Open Wide,

In This Universe, You Are My Guide.

What's Past Is Past, But Love Remains,

A Timeless Bond That Forever Sustains".

53. AFTER YOU

"Since You Left, Joy Feels Like A Distant Dream,

Each Day Stretches On, Lost In A Silent Scream.

Your Absence Wraps Around Me, A Heavy, Aching Weight,

I Wait For Your Return, For Love Can't Be Replaced.

No Other Soul Can Touch The Depths Of My Heart,

In A World Full Of Faces, You Were My Art.

I Turn Away From Others, For They Can't Ignite,

The Spark That You Brought, My Eternal Light.

Every Hour That Passes Is Filled With Your Name,

Time Stands Still In This Sorrowful Game.

I Hold Onto Memories, Both Sweet And Bittersweet,

Wishing For The Moment When Our Hearts Will Meet.

Here I Am , Lost In This Endless Night,

Hoping For A Dawn Where Everything Feels Right.

For A Love Like Ours Is Rare And Profound,

In This Quiet Longing, My Heart Is Unbound".

54. HEART'S DELIGHT

"Something In The Air Was Cold,

Something Of You Was In My Thoughts,

Something In The Air Was Cold, Yet Your Thoughts Warmed My Heart,

With Joy Mingling With Sorrow, A Bittersweet Work Of Art.

That Night Lingered, Half-past Midnight, Under The Full Moon's Glow,

The Moon, Reflecting Your Beauty, Made My Emotions Overflow.

In The Soft Shadows, You Stole Glances That Made Time Stand Still,

With Every Fleeting Look, My Heart Was Filled With A Thrill.

What Moments We Shared Felt Like A Dream Spun From Fate,

Your Laughter Echoed In My Soul, Making Me Yearn And Wait.

Even Now, When I Recall How You Gazed With Such Grace,

I Find Solace In Those Memories, Each One A Warm Embrace.

Can The Heart Truly Shine, Even When Shaped By Longing's Hand?

I Find Beauty In The Distance, As If By Fate We're Planned.

When I Couldn't Reach You, My Heart Felt Heavy And Bare,

Now, As You Turn To Look Back, My Spirit Dances In The Air.

I Craved Your Presence, A Bond I Couldn't Claim,

But Now, As I Pray, I Seek Your Heart's Warm Flame.

Your Words, Like Gentle Arrows, Shielded Me From Despair,

In Your Laughter, I Found Refuge, A Love Beyond Compare.

The Evening Breeze Carries Whispers, Like Secrets Shared Anew,

Each Gust Speaks Of My Longing, My Thoughts Forever True.

Here I Am , With Open Arms, Ready To Bridge The Divide,

With Every Heartbeat, I Hope You'll Be By My Side.

In This Dance Of Fate And Dreams, Let Our Souls Intertwine,

For In The Tapestry Of Love, Your Heart Is Forever Mine.

As The Stars Light The Night Sky, I Send My Wishes To You,

For Every Moment Apart Only Deepens This Love So True.

Let's Weave Our Stories Together, With Laughter And Light,

For In This Beautiful Journey, You Are My Heart's Delight".

55. BARREN LAND

"This Is How It Is: No Desire to Seek the State of My Heart
I Have No Thoughts Of You, Nor Of Myself;

My Heart, Like A Barren Land, Aches In Silence.

Oh Tree Of My Yearning, How Harsh This Autumn Is,

What Of The Bloom And The Fragrance?

Not Even A Trace Remains.

Inside Me Resides A Soul Once Full Of Purpose,

What's The Profit? What's The Loss?

Those Questions No Longer Linger.

The Hearts Wounded And The Lovers Intoxicated,

Peace And Debate? They Are Strangers Now, Lost In Time.

Look At My Courage; Grant Me This Mercy,

Desire For Perfection? Not Even A Shadow Of It Remains.

The Sanctuary Of My Gaze Lies In Ruins;

Today, The Horizon Wears A Shroud Of Despair.

Oh, This Cautious Atmosphere-Will We Ever Fly Free?

There's No Southern Breeze, Nor Northern Winds To Lift Us.

See How The Days And Nights Intertwine,

Yesterday, I Was Lifeless; Today, I Am Not Alive.

This Matter Of My Time And Wealth, It's A Riddle:

There's Neither The Dawn Of Separation Nor The Dusk Of Union.

Once, Beauty Was A Standard In Our Minds;

Now, Even Examples Of Beauty Have Vanished.

I Am A Curious Creature, So Strange Indeed,

I've Destroyed Myself, And Not A Single Regret Lingers".

56. RESTLESSNESS

"It's Not That I Lack The Words To Express My Sorrow,
But My Heart Resists, Unsure Of How To Reveal.
Even Now, I've Yet To Grasp The Reason Behind My
Restlessness,
For I Still Cannot Find The Courage To Speak To You.

My Heart Aches In Silence, Yet My Feelings Are Vast,
How Can I Share This Depth Without Sounding Foolish?
You Were Once The Language Of My Soul,
But Now, The World Feels Distant, Leaving Me Speechless.

We, The Humble Seekers, Are Without A Sanctuary,
There's No Refuge In Words That Could Reach You.
O God, Grant Mercy To This Aching Heart,
For It's Not Mere Tears, But The Absence Of Comfort I
Feel.

In That Forsaken Alley Where I Used To Wander,
Now Even My Own Shadows Refuse To Return To You.
Each Step Echoes The Distance Between Us,
A Love Unspoken, Waiting For The Moment To Break
Free".

The Promise of Loyalty Has Lost Its Chance:

"What Hope Remains To Recall Our Sacred Vow?
Do You Even Remember The Bond We Once Wove?

The Changing Seasons Stir Memories Anew,
How Swiftly Humans Can Change, How Fleeting We Are,
Your Life Was A Blessing, A Gift Bestowed In Your Name,
In Whatever Way I've Lived, It's All Owed To You.

My Heart Whispers, Perhaps You're Weary Too,
But What Can I Say Of My Heart? It Knows Nothing True.

Recall The Intoxication Of Our First Embrace,
Even Without Wine, Your Visage Was A Garden's Grace.

Now, We Find Ourselves In This Desolate State,
As The Veins Of The Wine Ignite Like The Fire In My Soul.

For Ages, I've Wandered With No Hope, No Light,
Yet My Heart Still Cries Out, Yearning To Be Known.

We Were So Naive, Thinking We Understood,

That Life's Pains Are Distinct From Love's Heavy Load.

Now, In This Gathering Of Friends, An Unfamiliar Glow,
Some Heads Bowed Low, Lost In Grief's Silent Throe.

Everyone I See Feels Like They're Bound In Chains,
This City Has Become A Prison Of Unending Pains.

Your Name May Seldom Grace My Verses' Flow,
Yet I Find My Sorrow Transforming Into New Shapes.

We Once Tamed The Harshness Of Seasons Gone Cold,
Unaware Of The Chill That True Separation Holds.

When Clarity Returned, All I Saw Were Broken Dreams,
Like Scattered Pages Of Restless Thoughts, Unexplained".

57. JOURNEY THROUGH CLOUDS

*"**My Dove**; Life Feels Like A Journey Through The Clouds,*
A Beautiful But Fleeting Dance In The Sky.
While Others Carve Out Their Homes On Earth,
We Wander, Searching, As The Moments Pass By.

Each Day Unfolds With Its Own Simple Joys,
But Somehow, I Find Myself Missing The Spark,
The Connection That Ignited Our Hearts,
In A World That Often Feels Cold And Stark.

Though Love Was Just A Whisper, A Brief, Bright Flame,
Its Memory Clings To My Soul Like A Song.

Those Precious Days-Four In Total-
Felt So Right, Yet They Slipped Away Too Long.

I Wonder, My Love, If We Could Capture
Even A Fragment Of Those Fleeting Hours,
To Build A World Where Time Stands Still,
A Sanctuary Adorned With Love's Sweet Flowers.

Let Us Not Let The Clouds Define Our Fate, But Weave
Our Dreams Into Something Bright.

Together, We Can Create A Home In Our Hearts,
Where Love Thrives In The Warmth Of Its Light".

58. DEAR

"How Can Someone Be So Wonderfully Dear?

How Can You Encompass Everything, My Dear?

Even When I Meet You, Sadness Lingers Still,

How Can I Endure Life Without You, Against My Will?

How Can Someone's Memory Keep Us Alive,

How Can A Single Thought Serve As Our Drive?

How Does The Wind Ignite Flames That Soar?

How Can Mere Words Feel Like Embers That Roar?

Who Is Truly Happy After Facing Life's Blows?

How Can One Cherish The Pain That One Knows?

How Can We Remain Bound To Just One Soul,

When That One Person Alone Makes Us Whole?"

59. TRANSCENDS DISTANCE

"As I Reflect On Our Journey, I Find Myself Captivated By The Very Essence Of Our Connection. The Conversation Of Love Has Blossomed Between Us, Spreading Like An Intoxicating Fragrance That Lingers In The Air.

You Welcomed Me Into Your World, Wrapping Me In Warmth And Acceptance That I Never Thought Possible. Yet, How Do I Convey The Sorrow Of Your Absence? It Is A Truth I Grapple With Daily-A Truth That Carries With It The Weight Of Disgrace, A Heavy Heart That Longs For Your Presence.

When You Placed Your Hand Gently On My Burning Forehead, I Felt An Indescribable Energy Coursing Through Me, A Touch That Reached Deep Into My Very Soul, Igniting A Fire That Burns For You Alone.

I Wish For Your World To Be As Vibrant As Your Heart, Thriving Amidst The Storms Of Life. Whatever Trials May Come During Those Long, Lonely Nights, I Hope You Find Solace And Strength, For You Are Worth Every Ounce Of Struggle.

No Matter Where Life Leads You, You Always Find Your Way Back To Me. This Simple Truth Brings Me Comfort, Even In My Defeats. It Reassures Me That Our Connection Transcends Distance And Time".

60. UNSPOKEN

"Let Some Words Remain Unspoken,
And Let Some Whispers Go Unheard.
If We Spill All That's In Our Hearts,
What Else Will Linger In This World?
If We Listen To Every Single Thought,
What Essence Will Still Be Left For Us?

Let The Unseen Quietude Embrace Us,
And Let The Vibrant Tapestry Of Life Unfold.
Keep A Window Slightly Ajar,
So The Light Of Mystery Can Seep Through.

In This Space Between Us, I Find Magic,
A Realm Where Our Souls Can Dance,
Where Unvoiced Feelings Add Depth To Our Bond,
Creating A Melody That Is Uniquely Ours.

Every Glance, Every Silence,
Holds A Story Waiting To Be Told.
In The Pauses, I See Our Dreams,
In The Unsaid, I Feel Our Love Grow Bold.

So Let Some Words Remain Unshared,
Let The Beauty Of The Unknown Linger.
In This Delicate Balance, We Find Our Truth,
For It's In The Quiet That Our Hearts Grow Fonder.

You Are The Light In My Uncharted World,
The Laughter In My Moments Of Stillness.
Together, We Craft A Love That Breathes,
A Connection That Thrives On The Unspoken,
A Treasure That Exists Beyond The Words.

Let Us Cherish This Beautiful Dance,
Where Silence Sings And Glances Spark.
In The Mystery Of Our Hearts, We Find Home,
Where Love Flourishes, Even In The Dark".

61. TESTAMENT TO THE LOVE

"Is It Necessary For Love To Be A Grand Spectacle,

When Meeting The One Who's Distant Feels Futile?

Just Surviving Isn't Living In Separation,

We Call It Existing, But It's Merely An Illusion.

Your Connection To The Sun Is Not Mine To Claim,

*Where Did You Find This Essence That Draws Us
Together?*

You Took Your Time Arriving, And It's Hard To Bear,

I Didn't Want To Endure This Loneliness Forever.

What A Drama It Is, Where Everyone Judges Me,

Yet They All Desire To Be Just Like Me.

Each Whisper, Each Glance, They Don't See The Pain,

They See The Surface But Don't Know The Strain.

I Long For Your Laughter, The Warmth Of Your Smile,

In The Theatre Of My Heart, I Await Your Arrival.

Why Must Love Be A Show, With Scripts That Confound,

When All I Seek Is The Solace Of Your Sound?

With Every Heartbeat, I Feel Your Essence Near,

Yet The Distance Between Us Grows Sharper Each Year.

If Only They Knew The Truth Of Our Connection,

That Love Is Not A Performance, But A Deep Reflection.

So I Pen These Lines, An Ode To Our Bond,

A Testament To The Love That Keeps Me Fond.

In Every Moment Of Silence, In Every Tear I Shed,

Know That My Heart Speaks The Words Left Unsaid.

Let's Transcend This Tamasha, Break Free From The Roles,

For In The Quiet Of Our Souls, Love Truly Consoles.

You Are My Sun, My Moon, My Guiding Star,

Together, We Can Rewrite The Script, No Matter How Far".

62. LOYALTY

"What Will She Say If She Ever Comes To Meet?
Now, She Won't Swear By Loyalty Anymore, That's For
Sure.

We Thought We Could Forget Her, Let Go Of The Past,
Yet She Believed I Could Never Forget, That I'd Always
Endure.

So Much Thought I Put Into This, But Not To This Extent,
She'll Become A Memory, A Dream, In My Sight she'll
Present.

Even Among Many, One Day She'll Feel So Alone,
She'll Search For Me In The Crowd But Won't Find Me;
I've Flown.

Fate May Bring Her Before Me Someday,
But She Won't Be The Same, Lost In Yesterday.

That Solitude She Once Carried Will Be Her Only Friend,
A Heart That Once Cherished Now Learning To Mend".

62. STIR MY HEART

"Why Do You Stir My Heart?
I've Moved On, Yet Here You Are,

Why Bring Back Those Tender Glances,
Those Whispered Secrets In The Dark?

You Awaken Memories Long Buried,
Of Forgotten Nights Beneath The Stars.

On This Rugged Path Of Life,
These Memories Bring No Solace.

What Chill Do You Seek In My Heart,
From The Rains Of A Bygone Era?

Look At My Weary Feet,
See The Fire Raining Upon My Head.

Each Drop, My Earth Has Thirsty For,
For A long Time, It Craves Your Touch.

This Journey Requires Both Yearning And Motion,
There Are Distant Destinations To Reach, My Companion.

I Never Turned My Back On Hope;
I, Too, Have A Heart That Longs For A Friend.

In The Bitter Trials Of Life,
Whenever Youth Flashes In My Mind,

A Vision Of Graceful Deer Appears,
And Then, Like A Dream, It Fades Away.

So, Why Do You Stir My Heart, My Love?
For In Your Memory, I Find Both Joy And Sorrow,
And Perhaps, Just Perhaps, A Path Back To You".

63. MAN YOU KNEW

"Love, I Long To Explain,
How Each Moment Feels Heavier,
The Laughter We Once Shared,
Now Echoes In My Memory's Chamber.

Days That Once Sparkled Bright,
Now Seem Shrouded In Shadow,
Your Smile, A Distant Light,
Yet I Grasp For It In Every Sorrow.

They Say I've Lost My Charm,
That The Joy Has Slipped Away,
But In Truth, It's Your Warmth
That Keeps The Darkness At Bay.

I Yearn To Be The Man You Knew,
The One Who Danced In The Rain,
To Laugh Without A Care,
To Let Go Of This Quiet Pain.

So Here I Stand, Open And Bare,
Hoping You See Through This Facade,
That Beneath The Surface, I Still Care,
And Love You More Than Words Can Laud.

Help Me Find My Way Back,
To The Heart That Once Knew No Fear,
For In Your Love, I Find My Track,
A Path That Leads Me Ever Near".

64. WEAK

"I Am Weak, Yet Not So Weak,
I Am Weak, But Not So Frail,
In The Depths Of My Heart, Love's Fire Will Prevail.
Though Shadows May Loom, And Storms May Rise,
I Stand Strong, For Your Love Is My Prize.

Break Me Not, Dear, With Harsh Words Or Disdain,
For My Spirit Is Fierce, Despite All The Pain.
In The Battles Of Life, I May Falter And Bend,
But For You, My Love, I Will Never End.

Your Laughter Is My Strength, Your Smile My Shield,
In The Garden Of Hope, Our Love Is Revealed.
So Come, Hold My Hand, Let Us Face The Night,
Together, My Love, We'll Conquer With Light.

In Moments Of Doubt, When The World Feels Unkind,
Remember My Heart, Forever Entwined.
I May Stumble And Fall, But I'll Rise Once More,
For Your Love Is The Anchor I Endlessly Adore.

So Break Me Not, For I Am Stronger Than You See,
In The Depths Of My Weakness, I'll Always Be Free.
Together We'll Soar, Like Birds In The Sky,
In Love's Tender Embrace, We'll Forever Fly".

65. INTO YOUR EYES

"I Ventured Into The Tavern, Seeking Solace,
Only To Find Wine Flowing All Around Me,
But It Was Not The Intoxicating Drinks That Captivated
Me.

No, I Fell Into A Deeper Trance-
Only When I Gazed Into Your Eyes,
Those Enchanting Eyes That Bloom Like Roses,
Filling My World With Their Vibrant Colours.

Each Time I Behold Your Image,
A Portrait Of Beauty And Grace,
I Realize That In Those Moments,
I Need No Words, No Verses To Express My Feelings.

Your Presence Alone Suffices;
You Are My Muse, My Inspiration.
In Your Eyes, I Discover My Poetry,
In Your Smile, I Find My Story.

With Every Glance, You Draw Me Deeper,
Into A Realm Where Only You And I Exist,
Where The Noise Of The World Fades,
And All That Remains Is The Melody Of Our Love.

So, My Love, Know This:
Even In The Midst Of Life's Distractions,
It Is You Who Holds My Heart,

You Who Turns My Mundane Moments Into Verses,
And Makes My Soul Dance In Joyous Abandon".

66. LOST MYSELF

"I Have Lost Myself
In Search of Someone!
Perhaps I May Never Reconnect With Who I Was!

In The Depths Of My Soul, I Wander,
Lost In The Echoes Of Your Laughter,

Every Moment Stretches Like An Eternity,
As I Search For You In Every Shadow,

In The Whispers Of The Wind,
And The Silence Of The Night.

I Have Become A Stranger To Myself,
A Reflection Shattered, Drifting,
Seeking The Warmth Of Your Presence,
The Comfort Of Your Touch,

Yet, With Each Passing Day,
I Fear Our Paths May Never Cross Again.

The World Feels Hollow Without You,
Like A Canvas Void Of Colour,
Each Heartbeat A Reminder
Of The Love That Once Ignited My Spirit.

I Search For Fragments Of Our Memories,
But They Slip Through My Fingers Like Sand.

If I Could Hold On To Just One Moment,
The Way Your Eyes Sparkled In The Sun,
Or How Your Smile Lit Up My Darkest Days, I Would
Cherish It Forever,
Yet I'm Left With The Ache Of Longing,
The Uncertainty Of What Could Have Been.

But Perhaps, In This Search For You,
I Might Discover Myself Anew,
For Love Transforms Us,
Even When It Feels Like We've Lost Our Way.

I'll Keep Looking, Through Every Heartache,
For The Hope That Love Will Lead Me Back To Both You
And The Person I Used To Be".

67.FATE TO SEPARATION

"When your Command Came, I Abandoned Love,
Yet My Heart, Despite That, Shuddered At The Thought Of
Separation.

How Do I Express My Longing For You?
Words Fail Me, As If Even The Meaning Has Revolted.

I Thought Those Who Leave Would Return,
But You Went And Turned My Fate To Separation.

Now, Even My Enemy's Intentions Evoke Love,
For Your Affection Has Made Love My Habit".

68. DAYS PASS

"Without A Plea, I Passed Through This Life,

What Joy is There Without Life's Strife?

All Keep Moving, Yet No One Knows,

When Does a Hunter Strike Without Foes?

In This Journey We Call Life , I Often Ponder,

How Can One Find Joy In Silence, In Wonder?

As Days Flow By, Each Moment A Thread,

Yet, So Many Wander Without A Word Said.

I Could Forget You, But Here Lies the Pain,

How Will My Days Pass Without Your Name?

Like Flickering Lights, Even in Wind's Chase,

I Shine On, Yet Need Your Warm Embrace.

Each Heartbeat Echoes Your Sweet, Tender Name,

In The Depths Of My Heart, It Burns Like A Flame.

Without Your Laughter, The World Feels So Grey,

You Are The Sun That Brightens My Day.

So, Let Me Pen Down These Feelings, My Dear,

For Every Second Without You Feels Unclear.

You Are The Reason My Spirit Can Soar,

The Melody Of Love That I Endlessly Adore.

In Your Absence, My Soul Feels A Void,

Every Thought Of You Makes My Heart Overjoyed.

Together, We Weave A Tapestry Of Dreams,

A Future So Bright, Bursting At The Seams.

In Every Moment, I Cherish Your Grace,

A Love So Profound, Time Cannot Erase.

Let's Journey Together, Through Joy And Through Strife,

For You Are My Heart, My Love, My Life".

68. DEVOID OF LIGHT

This Is How I Feel, My Love-Lost In A Landscape Devoid Of Light. Every Thought Of You Seems To Fade Like Petals In A Harsh Autumn Wind. Your Essence, Once Vibrant, Now Seems Like A Distant Memory. I Search For The Beauty We Once Shared, But All I Find Is Silence Where Laughter Used To Dwell.

Inside Me, Your Spirit Once Stirred Passion And Purpose, But Now I Grapple With Questions That Have Lost Their Meaning. What Is It To Gain Or To Lose When The Heart Feels Nothing? The Wounds Of Love Ache In Solitude, And The Debates Of Longing Have Ceased.

I Long For Your Presence, Your Warmth To Grant Me Strength. The Dreams Of Our Shared Perfection Have Dimmed, Leaving Behind Only Shadows. My Gaze, Once Filled With Hope, Now Wanders Through The Ruins Of What We Created Together.

In This Space Where Love Once Flourished, I Fear We Might Never Escape The Weight Of Our Uncertainty. The Winds That Once Carried Us Are Now Still, And I Find Myself Caught Between The Memories Of Yesterday's Joy And Today's Emptiness.

The Riddle Of Our Time Together Lingers In My Mind-Where Is The Dawn That Promised Unity? Where Is The Dusk That Promised Peace? The Beauty We Knew Seems Like A Ghost Haunting My Thoughts, And In This Quiet Agony, I Realize I Am A Strange Being. I've Embraced My Own Destruction, Yet In That Chaos, I Find No Sorrow-Only The Void That Your Absence Has Created.

69. LOST MY WAY

*"If You Would Just Trust Me A Little,
I Could Leap Across The Vast River,
My Heart Strong And Unwavering,
For Your Love Gives Me The Courage To Defy The
Impossible.*

*But In The Chaos Of Life, I've Lost My Way,
Drowning In The Noise And The Shadows,
Yearning For The Solace Only You Can Provide.*

*If I Could Embrace My Fate,
I Would Love You Fiercely, With All My Heart.*

*The Ache Of Separation Mirrors The First Moments Apart,
Each Day A Reminder Of Your Absence,
And Yet, I Hold On To The Hope That Lingers,
That Our Paths Will Cross Once More.*

*Every Heartbeat Whispers Your Name,
Every Sigh Is A Testament To My Longing.*

*In Dreams, Your Smile Lights Up My Darkness,
And With Each Dawn, I Am Haunted By The Memory Of
You.*

If You Could See How My Soul Aches,
How Every Moment Without You Feels Like Eternity,

You Would Understand That My Love Is Unwavering,
A Flame That Burns Brighter In Your Absence.

So, Trust Me, My Love, Just This Once,
Let's Bridge This Distance With Our Hearts, Turning
Chaos Into Harmony,
And Sorrow Into The Sweetest Joy.

Together, We Can Rewrite Our Story,
With Every Breath, I Promise To Love You Deeper,
For You Are My Muse, My Guiding Light,
The One I Will Cherish For All Time.

Let's Find Our Way Back To Each Other,
To The Warmth Of Our Shared Dreams,
For In Your Arms, I Am Whole,
And Our Love Will Conquer All".

70. RIVER OF SORROW

"When I Spoke Of My Sorrow, A River Flowed,

She Shed Tears, And The River Overflowed.

Everyone Had Verses For The River To Sing,

But I Was The One Who Embraced Its Sting.

In The Depths Of My Heart, I Poured Out My Pain,

Each Word A Drop That Fell Like Rain.

As I Spoke Of Love Lost And Dreams That Fade,

Her Eyes Mirrored The River, Where Memories Wade.

The World May Weave Tales Of Joy And Despair,

But Only I Knew The Depths Of Our Shared Air.

While Others Penned Verses Of Laughter And Light,

I Held The Weight Of Our Shadows, A Beautiful Plight.

With Every Heartbeat, My Longing Would Rise,

Like The River's Flow Beneath Vast, Open Skies.

Though The Currents May Pull And The Tides May Sway,

In Her Gaze, I Found The Strength To Stay.

For Love, In Its Essence, Is A River Profound,

It Carries Our Whispers, Our Hopes, And Our Sound.

And Though We May Wander Through Valleys Of Sorrow,

Together We'll Forge A Path To Tomorrow".

71. YOUR ABSENCE

"Though I Once Insisted That I Felt No Ties,
The Truth Emerged When You Stepped Away,
My Heart Began To Race, Consumed By Fear,
In The Silence Of Your Absence, I Found Dismay.

Each Moment Without You Felt Like A Lifetime,
Memories Of Your Laughter Echoed In My Mind,
I Realized My Love For You Ran Deep,
A Bond So Profound, In Your Essence I Was Entwined.

Your Quirks And Habits, Once Mere Observations,
Became Part Of My Every Thought And Prayer,
I Began To Mirror Your Gentle Laughter,
And Longed To Feel Your Warmth, Your Tender Care.

In Your Absence, I Discovered A Truth,
That My Heart Had Woven Itself Into Your Soul,
With Every Beat, It Echoed Your Name,
You Became My Muse, My Missing Whole.

So Here I Stand, Bare And True,
With Every Word, I Send My Heart To You,
For In Loving You, I've Found My Place,
In This Dance Of Souls, It's Your Love I Embrace".

72. WANDERER

*"When I Remember You, The World Seems To Stretch
Endlessly,
And Love Pulls Me Like A Mighty Mountain, Strong And
Steep.*

*May No Arrow Reach Me From The Hands Of My Foes,
For Now, It Is My Friend Who Draws The Bow Deep.*

*In Moments Of Leisure, Thoughts Of Old Friends Appear,
And When They Do, It Feels Like The Pulse Of My Very
Soul.*

*There's No Limit To This Love, No Greed That Binds Our
Hearts,
Let's See How Far We Can Go, Let Our Passions Unfold.*

*Like Threads Pulled Taut In The Fabric Of Fate,
We Drift In The Currents Of Time, Swept Away,
I Am But A Wanderer, Destined To Find My Way,
With You As My Compass, Guiding Me Day By Day.*

*You Are The Essence Of My Being, My Cherished Delight,
In Your Presence, I Am Whole; Without You, I Am Lost.*

Together, We Weave Dreams, Transcending The Night,
In This Dance Of Our Hearts, We Embrace Every Cost.

So Let The World Around Us Stretch And Bend,
As Long As You're With Me, Love, I Will Never Break.

In The Journey Of Existence, We Write Our Own Song,
For In Your Arms, My Dear, Is Where I Truly Belong".

73. CONFESSION

"I Feel That Perhaps I've Dared To Reveal,
Is There Any Complaint You Hold Against Me?
For I Have Undeniably Fallen In Love With You.

In This World, Where No One Finds Their True Desire,
Some Never Found Us, And We Couldn't Find You.

We Both Knew This Love Was A Distant Dream,
Yet You Spoke Your Truth, And I Couldn't Help But
Confess Mine".

74. WHAT WILL YOU SAY

"What Will She Say If She Ever Comes To Meet?
I Wonder If She'll Still Hold That Warmth In Her Voice,
Or If The Silence Will Linger, A Reminder Of Our Defeat,
A Testament To Choices, To Paths That Weren't Our
Choice.

Once, We Painted Dreams On The Canvas Of Our Nights,
Believing Love Would Conquer, That Time Wouldn't Tear
Apart,
But Now, I Ponder If She Recalls Those Endless Heights,
Or If She's Moved On, With A New Flame In Her Heart.

I thought I Could Forget, That Her Memory Would Fade,
Yet, Here I Stand, Haunted By Moments We Shared,
With Every Breath, I Feel The Love That Won't Degrade,
As If Her Essence Still Lingers, And I Am Still Ensnared.

She'll Remember Me As A Whisper, A Flicker Of The Past,
Searching For Solace In A World Where I Once Stood,
Amongst The Crowd, A Fleeting Glance, Shadows Cast,
Yet, In Her Solitude, She'll Find Nothing That Feels Good.

So If Fate Allows Our Paths To Cross Again,
I Hope She Sees The Changes, The Growth In My Soul,
For Though The Love May Have Dimmed, It's Echo
Remains,A Gentle Reminder That Love, Even In Absence,
Can Console.

What Will She Say When Memories Flood Back Like The
Tide?
Will She Acknowledge The Beauty, The Laughter, The
Pain?
Or Will She Turn Away, With Pride Tucked Inside,
A Stranger Now, In A Dance That We Can't Regain?

In This Vast Universe, Filled With Chances Untold,
I Await The Moment, The Spark Of Our Reunion,
To Share Not Just Nostalgia But The Love That's Grown
Bold,
And Perhaps Together, We'll Rewrite Our Own
Conclusion".

75. ECHO OF YOUR ABSENCE

"When The Echo Of Your Absence came, I Set Aside My Love, Believing It Was For The Best. But Even As I Tried To Move On, My Heart Trembled At The Mere Thought Of Losing You.

How Can I Articulate This Longing That Consumes Me? Each Word I Try To Express Feels Inadequate, As If Even The Very Essence Of Meaning Has Conspired Against Me.

I Once Thought That Those Who Leave Would Find Their Way Back, That We Would Reunite Under The Stars Like Before. But You Chose A Path That Led Away From Me, Leaving My Fate Entwined With This Unbearable Separation.

Now, As I Navigate This World Without You, Even The Intentions Of My Enemies Remind Me Of Love. Your Memory Lingers, Turning Every Moment Into A Bittersweet Reminder Of What We Had.

Your Love Has Become My Routine, My Habit, And With Every Heartbeat, I Find Myself Yearning For You More.

In Your Absence, I've Come to Realize That Love Is Not Just A Feeling-It's An Existence, An Essence That You Brought Into My Life.

You've Woven Yourself Into The Very Fabric Of My Being, And No Matter How Far Apart We Are, My Heart Will Always Call For You."

76. REGRETS

"In Love, Regrets Are An Inescapable Truth,

For Even The Closest Friends Can Be Blind.

It Was Only Because I Trusted You So Deeply,

That Even Without Complaints, Surprises Still Wound Me.

What Can I Say About The Sorrow I Carry,

Except That This Is Life; It's Filled With Heartaches.

I Have Forgotten The Anguish Of Your Absence,

For In The Hearts Of Those Who Love,

Loneliness Is A Familiar Companion"

77. KINDNESS

"Please, Show Me A Little Kindness. In This Whirlwind Of Emotions We Call Love, I Find Myself Yearning To Understand Its True Essence. What Does It Mean To You? How Does It Shape Your Heart And Soul?

I Often Feel Lost In The Chaos Of My Own Thoughts And Troubles, And Sometimes, I Find It Difficult To Navigate Through This Storm Alone.

Can You Share Your Burdens With Me? Open Up About What Weighs On Your Heart, So I Can Stand By You, Support You, And Ease Your Pain As You Do For Me.

Together, Let's Explore The Depths Of Our Feelings. Let's Find Solace In Each Other's Presence, Transforming Our Worries Into A Bond That Grows Stronger Every Day.

Your Happiness Means Everything To Me, And I Want To Be The One You Can Lean On, Just As You Are My Anchor."

78. LOVE I ONCE KNEW

"My Dove, Don't Seek The Love I Once Knew,
For In You, I Discovered A Truth So Profound.

When You Are Near, The Sun Paints The Sky Anew,
Your Laughter, Like A Melody, A Sweet, Enchanting Sound.

With Your Absence, The World Feels Heavy And Grey,
Your Smile Ignites A Spark In The Dullest Day.

You Are My Spring, Bringing Warmth To My Soul,
Without You, My Heart Feels An Endless Toll.

In Your Gaze, I See Dreams Yet To Unfold,
A Tapestry Of Moments, Precious And Bold.

If Only You Knew The Depth Of My Care,
In Your Presence, I Find Solace Beyond Compare.

Life Holds Many Trials Beyond Love's Sweet Strife,
Yet None Could Match The Beauty You Bring To My Life.

So Let Us Weave Our Dreams, Through Laughter And
Tears,
For In This Shared Journey, I'll Cherish You Through The
Years."

"Don't Ask Me For The Love I Once Gave, My Beloved,
I Thought If You Are With Me, Life Is Radiant.

If Your Sorrow Is Present, What Is The Burden Of The World?
Your Beauty Brings Life To The Blossoms Of Spring.

What Is There In This World Besides Your Eyes?
If I Have You, Then Destiny Would Be Fulfilled.

It Wasn't Like This; I Only Wished For It To Be So
There Are Other Sorrows In The World Besides Love,
There Are Other Joys As Well, Apart From The Joy of Union".

79. DEVOTED TO YOU

"In A World Where Love Often Feels Fleeting, My Heart Finds Its True Home Only With You. No Matter How Tumultuous The Seas Of Life May Be, I Envision Us Navigating Together, In The Same Boat, Anchored By Our Dreams And Desires.

I Am Devoted To You; I Would Gladly Dedicate My Life To Serving At Your Doorstep, Cherishing Every Moment Spent In Your Presence.

Your Streets, Vibrant With Memories And Hopes, Represent Our Shared Future-Where Each Alley Holds A Promise Of Love And Every Corner Whispers Tales Of Us.

Together, We'll Create A Life Filled With Laughter, Understanding, And Unwavering Support. You Are Not Just My Love; You Are My Destiny, The Guiding Light That Illuminates My Path."

80. THE ACHE OF SEPARATION

"In The Intricate Dance Of Our Relationship, I Often Find Myself Reflecting On The Moments Of Regret That Arise. It's A Natural Part Of Love, Isn't It? Even The Closest Friends Can Falter In Their Understanding.

I Trusted You So Completely, Perhaps Too Much, And That Trust Has Woven Both Joy And Sorrow Into The Fabric Of My Heart.

Even In Silence, When I Hold Back My Grievances, Life Has A Way Of Unveiling Unexpected Truths. I Cannot Help But Wonder About The Roots Of My Sadness; It Seems Woven Into The Very Essence Of Existence. Life, With Its Trials And Tribulations, Teaches Us Lessons We Never Anticipated.

Though I've Tried To Push Aside The Pain Of Your Absence, There Are Moments When It Surges Back, Reminding Me Of What I Miss.

I Know That, Like Many Who Love Deeply, I Often Find Myself In Moments Of Solitude, Feeling The Weight Of Longing And The Ache Of Separation".

"My Heart Was The Snow Where You Left Your Mark.

You're Always In My Thoughts, Even When You' Aren't Here."

"Loving Me Feels Like Embracing Heartbreak, As That's A Part Of Who I Am. My Heart Is Worn On My Sleeve, And It Yearns To Chase After You, Yet I Fear The Consequences Of Love. My Heart Resists Love, But It Also Aches For It."

147

"What Good Is This Heart If It Cannot Be With The One It Beats For?

81. LOVED YOU

"If You Ever Miss Me, Know That I Have Loved You In Sentences And Silences, Prose And Poetry, Thunderstorms And The Peace That Eventually Comes. I Have Loved You More Than I Have Loved The Ones Who Have Loved Nobody More Than Me.

I Have Loved You On Days When My Heart Was Blooming And On Days When It Was Breaking. I Have Loved You With The Kind Of Sincerity That Can Make Anyone Wonder What They Have Done To Deserve A Love Like That. It Was You Who Couldn't Value It, Any Of It."

82. FIRST LINE

"If You Ever Return, The First To Meet You Will Be Me,

In That Very Place Where Paths Intertwine And Hearts Are Free.

Should A Battle Arise, In Your Name, For Love's True Call,

I'll Stand Undaunted, Leading The Line, Ready To Risk It All.

In The Quiet Corners Of My Heart, Where Memories Reside,

I'll Cherish Every Moment, Every Tear We've Cried.

With Every Step I Take, I'll Journey Through The Night,

Until The Dawn Reveals Your Face, My Guiding Light.

No Fear Shall Hold Me Back; Your Love Is My Strength,

Through Storms And Shadows, I'll Go Any Length.

For In Your Eyes, I Find My Home, My Sacred Space,

And In This Endless Longing, I'll Forever Chase Your Grace.

So If Fate Brings You Near, My Heart Shall Be Your Throne,

Together, We'll Weave Dreams, No Longer Alone.

In Every Whispered Promise, In Every Gentle Sigh,

With You, My Love, I'll Soar, As If Destined To Fly".

83. NO ONE

"No One Came to My Heart's Woe,
No One Came, My Love,
No One At All!

Footsteps Have Faded Into Distant Paths,
The Night Has Fallen, Scattering The Stars Glow,
Dream-Laden Lamps Flicker, Unsteady In The Hall,
Every Path Has Quieted, Every Journey Stilled.

Strangers Have Dimmed Their Footsteps,
Leaving Only Traces In The Dust,
While The Candles Of Hope Burn Low,
Raise The Cups Of Wine, Fill Them To The Brim,
Let's Indulge In Dreams That Are Ours To Keep,
For Now, Here, There's No One Left…
No One To Come Anymore!

*"I Will Wait For You, No Matter How Long It Takes,
Either You Come To Me, Or I Shall Fade Into Oblivion."*

*My Beloved, The Depth Of My Yearning For You Is Beyond
Words. Each Passing Moment Without You Feels Like An
Eternity. I Want You To Know That I Am Here,
Unwavering In My Commitment, Waiting For The Day You
Choose To Be By My Side.*

*This World May Spin And Change, But My Heart Remains
Steadfast In Its Devotion. I Promise To Hold Onto Hope,
To Cherish The Memories We've Made, And To Dream Of
The Future We Could Share.*

*So, I'll Keep Looking For Signs Of Your Arrival, While
Embracing The Thought That Even If You Don't Come, I
Will Find Solace In The Love I Hold For You. Until Then,
My Heart Will Patiently Wait, Longing For The Moment
We Are United Again.*

84. LONELINESS

"In A Small Village Once,
Where The Lights Were Few And Shadows Long,
There Stood Many Trees, Yet So Few Homes,
Separated By Distances That Felt So Strong.

The Loneliness There Was Vast And Deep,
In That Silence, My Heart Would Often Keep,
A Sense Of Yearning, An Old, Worn Ache,
In Those Quiet Moments, My Thoughts Would Break.

I Could Ponder The Old Sorrows That Lingered,
In My Heart's Corners, They Gently Fingered,
In Such A World, Love Would Find Its Way,
Whispers Of You Would Softly Sway.

In Every Thought, Your Essence Would Appear,
A Dream So Vivid, Yet So Unclear,
The Mysteries We Held, Beyond Mere Sight,
How Do I Show You My Love In The Night?

Even Dreams Have Limits, Boundaries To Cross,
But For You, My Dear, I'd Bear Any Loss.
Each Heartbeat A Step Towards Your Embrace,
In This Endless Journey, I Seek Your Grace.

So Here I Stand, With Love That Won't Fade,
In The Shadows, Our Memories Are Made.
Together We'll Light Up The Dark,
Two Souls Entwined, Igniting A Spark."

85. COME ONCE MORE

"Oh, Come Once More, Even If It's Just To Stir The Aching In My Heart.
Your Absence Has Carved A Void That Echoes Through My Days,
And I Find Myself Yearning For The Warmth Of Your Presence.
I Miss The Laughter We Shared, The Whispers In The Night,
So Come, If Only To Remind Me Of The Love We Once Knew.

Keep Alive Some Trace Of Our Love's Gentle Flame,
For Without You, I Wander Through Shadows Of What Could Have Been.
Each Moment Apart Has Stretched Like An Eternity,
Yet My Heart Still Believes That There's A Way Back To You.

Though Our Ties May Have Frayed, Let's Find A Way To Reconnect,
To Honour The Beauty Of Our Shared Memories, Even If Fleeting.
Who Will I Confide In About The Pain Of This Separation?
If You're Angry, Then Come Back, Just To Feel Our Connection Once More.

*For Ages Now, I've Been Deprived Of The Solace That
Comes From Tears,
Oh, My Comfort, My Life! Return To Me And Bring Your
Sadness,
For In Your Presence, Even Grief Feels Like A Tender
Embrace.
These Last Flickering Lights Of Our Love-I Hold Them
Close,
Don't Let Them Fade Into Darkness; I Still Believe In Us.*

*So Come, If Only To Share A Moment, A Smile, A Sigh,
Let's Weave Together The Threads Of Our Story Once
Again,
And Maybe, Just Maybe, We Can Find A Way Back To
Love."*

86. NOISE

"In Your Surroundings, There Was Noise
In Your Surroundings, There Was So Much Noise,
My Words Were Lost, Caught In The Void,
I Could Not Speak, Nor Could You Hear,
My Feelings Lingered, Unvoiced, Unclear.

Beneath Your Windows, Flowers Bent Low,
They Gazed At Us, While Time Moved Slow.
On Your Roof, The Moon Chose To Stay,
Yet Still, My Words Drifted Away.

I Thought, In Your Presence, My Heart Would Sing,
But Fear Kept My Tongue From Whispering.
So The Truth Remained, Silent And Gray,
My Emotions Held Captive, My Words In Dismay."

87. IN HER WORLD

"In Her World, I Did Not Reside,

Yet Within Her, I Lingered Deep Inside.

Stars And Moon In Her Tresses Gleamed,

Like A Cloud, I Drifted, Dreamed And Dreamed.

Even Though I Was Absent From Her Reality,

In The Quiet Corners Of Her Heart, I Found My Sanctuary.

Her Laughter Echoed Like A Celestial Song,

In The Depths Of Her Eyes, Where I Felt I Belonged.

And Those Desolate Eyes, So Full Of Pain,

Once, Long Ago, I Knew Them Well, Again And Again.

A Place Of Solitude, Yet Filled With Light,

In Every Tear, I Saw Our Shared Night.

I Remember The Warmth Of Her Gaze,

How It Wrapped Around Me, Like A Comforting Haze.

Each Glance Held Stories, Whispered Dreams,

In The Silence, Our Love Flowed In Streams.

In The Garden Of Thoughts Where Memories Grow,

I Plant My Hopes, So She'll Always Know.

Though Miles Apart, My Heart Remains,

Bound To Her Spirit, Through Joys And Pains.

For Every Moment We've Yet To Share,

I Carry Her Essence, Everywhere.

In The Tapestry Of Stars, In The Dusk's Gentle Sigh,

Our Love, A Timeless Whisper, Will Never Die.

This Poem Is A Promise, A Heartfelt Plea,

That Even In Distance, She Is Part Of Me.

No Matter The Worlds That Keep Us Apart,

She Will Always Dwell In The Chambers Of My Heart."

86. DESTINED

"Not Everyone Is Destined To Find Their Goal,

But Life Is A Journey; It's The Path We Stroll.

So Let Us Walk Together, Hand In Hand,

Through The Twists And Turns Of This Vast Land.

You, Like A Lamp, Light The Way So Bright,

Guiding Me Through Shadows, Turning Dark To Light.

In Every Struggle, In Every Trial We Face,

Your Warmth And Your Laughter Fill The Empty Space.

The Destination May Be Uncertain, This Much Is True,

But With You By My Side, I Can Embrace The View.

Let's Cherish The Moments, Both Joyous And Tough,

For It's Not Just The End, But The Journey That's Enough.

In The Depths Of Despair, When The World Feels Cold,

Your Love Is A Story That Never Grows Old.

Together We'll Turn Every Sorrow To Grace,

Transforming Each Dark Hour Into A Warm Embrace.

So Let's Walk This Path, My Dear, You And I,

With Dreams In Our Hearts And Hope In The Sky.

For In Every Step, In Every Breath We Take,

We'll Create A Beautiful World, With Love As Our Stake."

87. YOUR BEAUTY

"Not Just A Face To Be Hidden,

But A Picture To Be Shared,

Who Shall I Show This Beauty To?

Your Beauty Isn't Just A Fleeting Glance,

It's A Portrait That Deserves The World's Dance.

Every Feature Tells A Story, Every Smile A Song,

In Your Presence, My Heart Feels It Belongs.

Your Eyes, Like Stars, Light Up The Night,

Drawing Me Closer, Filling Me With Delight.

Your Laughter, A Melody, A Sweet Serenade,

In A World Full Of Noise, You're My Calm, My Shade.

I Wish To Capture Each Moment We Share,

To Hold Your Hand And Show You I Care.

Not Just In Whispers, But In Shouts Of Love,

You're The Gift I've Prayed For, Sent From Above.

So Let's Not Hide This Magic, Let It Shine,

In The Canvas Of Life, Your Heart Intertwined With Mine.

For Every Glance, Every Touch, Every Breath We Take,

Is A Masterpiece Waiting, A Love We'll Create."

88. BARREN HEART

"I Never Sought Your Gaze, Though My Heart Ached For It. My Lips Remained Sealed, A Silent Testament To My Love For You. In Crowded Rooms, My Feelings Went Unnoticed; I Kept My Silence, Just As You Did, Both Of Us Bound By An Unspoken Pact.

Our Bond Runs So Deep, Yet It Feels Like A Chasm. What Sorrow Can Be Yours For A Heart That Never Sought You Out? Isn't It Enough That We Both Cling To This Illusion Of Connection? You Never Offered A Word Of Solace, And I Never Dared To Ask For It.

With Every Encounter, I Held My Thirst In Check, Constrained By The Decorum Of Our Surroundings. Even The Simplest Gestures, Like A Fleeting Glance, Seemed Out Of Reach, As If The Very Air Around Us Conspired To Keep Us Apart.

I Carry My Sorrows Like A Cloak, Hidden From The World, Never Showing My Wounds In The Bustling Marketplace Of Life.

O Gentle Rain Of My Affections, Will You Not Wash Over This Barren Heart? Have You Never Felt The Urge To Nourish What Lies Dry And Forgotten? Like A Steadfast Guardian, I Stood Still, Waiting For A Sign, While My Heart Remained Quiet, Yearning For A Movement That Never Came.

If You Have Forgotten Me, Can I Truly Blame You? For I Too Have Shied Away From The Courage Of Connection, Never Reaching Out, Afraid Of The Silence That Might Follow.

But Know This: My Heart Is A Garden, Waiting For Your Touch, Longing For The Moment Our Paths May Finally Converge. Until Then, I Remain Here, Silent And Hopeful, Caught In The Delicate Balance Of Love Unspoken."

89.BETRAYAL

"In The Shadows Of Our Suffering
You Bear The Weight Of Your Own Sorrows,
Yet On My Heart, Your Pain Still Lingers,
When I Began To Speak Of Betrayal's Tale,
Suddenly, Your Memory Embraced Me,
I Never Wished To Falter In This Battle,
Yet My Shield Slipped, Lost In This Storm.

We Have Arrived At The Heart Of Our Fate,
Though It Was You Who Cast The Net Of Despair,
Neither Of Us Sought To Recount Our Story,
But Even So, You Asked About My Heart's Ache.

In Your Absence, Silence Wrapped Around Me,
Echoes Of Laughter Turned To Whispers Of Longing,
Every Moment Spent Apart Feels Like An Eternity,
Your Name Dances On My Lips, A Tender Sigh.

If Only You Could See The World Through My Eyes,
The Colours Dull Without Your Vibrant Presence,
Each Sunrise Reminds Me Of Your Warmth,
And Every Star Reflects The Light Of Your Soul.

As I Walk Through Memories, I Find You Everywhere,
In The Gentle Breeze And The Rustling Leaves,
In Every Song That Carries Your Essence,
You Are The Melody That Lingers In My Heart."

90. LORD

"I Find Myself Turning To You, O Lord, Because I Need Your Help. My Heart Aches For Her-The One I Cherish-Who Has Wandered Away.

I Miss Her Smile, Her Laughter, And The Warmth She Brought Into My Life. "A Soul Has Gone From Your Door, Distressed," And I Feel Lost Without Her.

Please, Bring Her Back To Me. Let Her See How Much I Love Her And How Much She Means To Me. I Believe That With Your Guidance, We Can Find Our Way Back To Each Other."

"In The Stillness Of Dawn;

Only One Dawn Brings Its Gentle Light,

Spreading Warmth Across The Courtyard Bright.

The Colours Of The Season Dance With The Breeze,

Stirring Dust In The Streets, Like Whispered Pleas.

Papers Flutter Like Dreams Upon The Ground,

While Dust Settles Softly, A Silence Profound.

How Cruel Is The Thought Of Your Face,

It Lingers In My Mind, Time Cannot Erase.

I Ponder Through The Night, Lost In Your Memory,

What Is It About Your Absence That Stirs This Reverie?

The Trees Have Fallen Asleep, Yet The Fragrance Wakes,

Life Shows Me Dreams, For Love's Sweet Sake.

In The Void Of Your Loyalty, Why Do Desires Ache?

What's Left Of This Home As Each Piece Starts To Break?

Every Day Brings A Loss, A Little More Despair,

Who Will Care For This Heart, Now Stripped Bare?

91. DEATH

"Your Absence Is A Veil That Shrouds My Heart,

Without It, What Would My World Be Like?

If I Were To Cry, Would The Heavens Not Break,

And Pour Down Like A Waterfall, Reflecting My Ache?

Death Itself Resides Within My Grasp,

For Your Sake, I'd Conquer Even That Final Gasp.

What Is The Meaning Of Parting's Cruel Embrace?

When Love's Essence Defies Time And Space.

In Every Moment Without You, I Feel The Sting,

Your Memory, A Melody That Forever Will Sing.

Life Is But A Shadow When You're Not Near,

Each Heartbeat A Reminder Of My Deepest Fear.

So Here I Stand, With My Heart In Hand,

Waiting For The Moment When You Understand.

That In This Dance Of Fate, I'd Brave Any Storm,

For Your Love Is The Light That Keeps My Soul Warm."

92. PRIDE

"In Your Gaze, My Pride Slipped Away,

A Quiet Command That Led My Heart Astray.

Those Captivating Eyes, Like A Gentle Tide,

Dissolved My Defences, Left My Ego Behind.

Before You, I Felt Fierce, Ready To Stand Tall,

With Dreams To Conquer, Believing I Could Have It All.

Yet Your Absence Has Shown Me A Truth So Clear,

That Love Can Move Mountains, And It Draws Me Near.

Had It Not Been For Your Enchanting Charm,

I Would Have Faced The World, Confident And Warm.

But Without You, I've Learned To Let Go,

To Embrace My Vulnerability, To Truly Let Love Show.

Now, I Stand Here, Hoping You'll See,

That My Heart Is Still Yours; You're The One Who Completes Me.

In Your Eyes, I Found The Strength To Mend,

And I Long For The Day We Can Begin Again.

So Here I Am, Reaching Out, Hoping You'll Feel,

The Depth Of My Love, The Sincerity That's Real.

Let The World Watch; Let It Say What It May,

For With You, I Know I Can Find My Way."

"In Your Name;

I Cannot Resist What Nature Has Inscribed,

Nor Can I Change The Fate That Has Arrived.

If Dark Days Were To Come, I Would Take The Blame,

But Instead, My Love, You Hold My Heart Aflame.

Your Words Carry A Weight Far Beyond Mere Sound,

In Each Whisper And Sigh, Profound Beauty Is Found.

I Cannot Express All That Your Presence Brings,

For In Your Essence, My Soul Truly Sings.

If I Could Rewrite The Script Of Our Days,

I Would Weave In The Joy, In Countless Ways.

"In Your Name;

ME IN YOUR LONGING

No Storm Could Overshadow The Light In Your Eyes,

For With You By My Side, The World Feels So Right.

So Here, My Beloved, I Vow To Remain,

To Cherish Each Moment, To Honour The Pain,

For Every Challenge That We Might Face,

I Will Stand By You, With Unwavering Grace.

Let The Winds Of Fate Blow As They May,

In The Garden Of Love, Together We'll Stay.

With You, I Am Whole, With You, I Am Free,

In This Beautiful Journey, Just You And Me."

93. YOUR TROUBLES

"I Won't Add To Your Troubles; I'll Quietly Depart,

Hiding My Sorrow Deep Within My Heart,

But My Love For You I Cannot Hide.

Let Me Linger A Moment At Your Door,

As Soon As I Regain My Consciousness I'll Be On My Shore,

Let Me Linger A Moment, Just To See Your Face,

In The Quiet Of My Heart, You Hold A Sacred Place.

These Moments Mean Everything, I'll Cherish Them Dear,

Each Glance And Every Whisper, I Keep You Near.

Like A Child With His Toys, Memories That Shine Bright,

You're The Warmth In My Heart, My Endless Light.

Though Distance May Part Us, My Love Will Remain,

Every Heartbeat Whispers, A Sweet, Gentle Refrain.

I'll Wait For Your Return, Through The Long, Lonely Nights,

For You Are My Beacon, My Hope, My Delights.

Know That I Love You, No Matter The Time,

In The Silence Between Us, Your Spirit Will Rhyme.

With Every Thought Of You, My Heart Will Stay True,

I'll Be Here, Always, Waiting For You."

94. CONFESSION-II

"My Love Remains Incomplete,
A Tale That's Yet To Unfold.
My Feelings Linger, Half-Formed,
While My Dreams, Like Fragile Vessels, Hold.

The Stories Of Love Rest On My Lips,
Yet They Remain Untold, Just Whispers In The Air.
An Entire World Of Incompleteness Surrounds Me,
Yet Amidst It All, I Stand Laid Bare.

With Every Truth That Colours My Heart,
I Embrace The Depths Of My Soul's Yearning.
Through The Shadows Of Doubt And Fear,
My Love For You, A Fire Still Burning.

I Acknowledge All That Is Unfulfilled,
Yet Still, I Lay My Heart At Your Feet.
For In This Incomplete Tapestry Of Life,
It's You, My Love, Who Makes Me Complete.

In The Silence, I Confess My Truth,
With Every Beat, I Draw You Near.
Though My Journey May Seem Half-Written,
It's Your Love That I Hold Dear."

95. BACK THEN

"Why Didn't You Find Me Back Then,
When Our Hearts Yearned To Be Adorned?
In The Days When Life Was A Canvas,
And Dreams Were Waiting To Be Born.

We Held The Passion Of Living Bright,
Yet I Nurtured A Longing So Deep,
To Taste The Sweetness Of Love's Embrace,
Even In Shadows Where Secrets Sleep.

In Those Moments, So Full Of Hope,
Our Souls Could Have Danced Through The Night,
But Instead, I Cherished A Wish To Endure,
While Holding On To A Longing For Light.

Oh, My Love, If Only Time Had Aligned,
We Could Have Crafted Our Own Fate,
But Now I Weave These Words With Care,
For The Love We Missed Can Still Resonate.

I Am Here With My Heart In Hand,
Yearning For The Chance To Make It Right,
For The Love We Lost Is Still Alive,
Waiting To Ignite In The Still Of The Night."

96. NOTHING WITHOUT YOU

"How Do I Express The Depth Of My Feelings For You?
Every Beat Of My Heart Sings Your Name;
Every Breath I Take Is Filled With Your Essence.
You Are The Music That Fills My Life,
A Beautiful Symphony That Brings Joy To My Soul.

When I Think Of You, I Think Of Light-
You Brighten My Darkest Days,
And Your Presence Refreshes My Spirit.
You Embody Every Happiness I Seek,
And You Are The Love That Colours My World.

In My Eyes, You Shine Like A Thousand Stars;
In My Memories, You Are Etched Like A Cherished
Photograph.
In My Dreams, You Are The Sweetest Vision,
The One I Long To Hold Close,
Even In Sleep, You Bring Me Peace.

You Are In My Every Word,
Filling My Conversations With Warmth And Affection.
You Define My Days And My Nights,
Creating A Rhythm That Dances Through My Thoughts.

To Be With You Is To Know Joy;
To Be Apart Feels Like Losing My Very Self.
Your Laughter Echoes In My Heart,
And Your Sadness Weighs On My Soul.

In Every Moment, In Every Heartbeat,
You Are The One I Cherish.
Wherever I Go, I Carry You With Me,
In Every Thought, In Every Heartbeat,
You Are My Constant, My Anchor.

How Do I Convey This Love, This Truth?
Without You, I Am Nothing-
A World Without Light, A Life Without Meaning."

97. MIRAGE

*"Is It A Mirage, A Deception, Or A Waterfall That You
Are?
In The Desert Of My Heart, A Thirst Remains-It's You, My
Star.*

*I Am But A Wandering Verse, Lost In The Expanse Of My
Own Pain,
An Echo From The Void, Whispering Your Name.*

*The Door Stands Ajar, As If Connected To My Very Soul,
A Knock On My Heart Speaks Of Longing-Your Presence
Makes Me Whole.*

*I Am A Shadow Tangled In The Warmth Of The Sun,
You Are The Promise Of Dusk, The Day's Gentle Run.*

*Even In My Being, It Feels Like I Am Not Truly Here,
You, My Love, Seem Distant, Yet So Vividly Near.*

*I Ponder The Fabric Of Our Reality, Stitched By Fate's
Hand,
In Every Heartbeat, In Every Silence, It's You I
Understand.*

*So Tell Me, Are You Real, Or A Dream That I Chase?
In This Whirlwind Of Emotions, I Find My Solace In Your
Grace.*

Though I Stand Alone, Surrounded By Night's Embrace,
I Carry You Within Me, In Every Time And Space.

You Are My Reason, My Muse, The Rhythm In My Heart,
A Symphony Of Love That Shall Never Depart.

In Every Thought, In Every Breath, My Devotion Flows,
For In This Vast Universe, It's Only You That I Chose."

2 Am Thoughts:

"If You Were Here,
If You Were Here, How Different Life Would Be,
You Would Say This, And You Would Say That,
You'd Be Amazed By The Little Wonders Around,
Your Laughter Would Fill The Air, Brightening Each
Moment.

If You Were Here, Everything Would Change,
Every Glance Would Spark A New Joy,
In Your Presence, Even Silence Would Speak,
Our Souls Would Dance In The Shared Stillness.

I Often Find Myself Lost In Thoughts Of You,
Imagining The Warmth Of Your Hand In Mine,
Wishing To Share Whispers In The Night,
And Dreams That Stretch Beyond The Stars.

In My Solitude, I Ponder These Moments,
The Conversations We'd Have, The Stories We'd Tell,
The Way You'd Bring Colour To My Dullest Days,
How You'd Turn The Mundane Into Something Magical.

If You Were Here, The World Would Feel Right,
Every Heartbeat Echoing The Rhythm Of Your Name,
And Together, We'd Create A Tapestry Of Memories,
Threaded With Laughter, Love, And Unspoken
Understanding.

I Often Talk With My Loneliness,
About These Very Things…!

98. MY ADORATION

"When I Think Of You, Sleep Eludes Me, As If The Very Thought Of You Ignites A Fire Within My Heart. How Could I Ever Close My Eyes When Your Presence Lingers In My Mind, Brightening My Every Thought? It Feels Almost Disrespectful To Seek Rest When There Is So Much Beauty To Ponder In You.

Even When I Attempt To Articulate The Depths Of My Feelings, The Words Often Fail Me. It's As If My Heart Races, Desperate To Share Its Truth, Yet The Language Of Love Sometimes Escapes.

The Tears That Gather In My Eyes Are Not Just Of Sorrow; They Are A Reflection Of The Overwhelming Joy You Bring Into My Life. Each Drop Is A Testament To My Affection, An Echo Of The Feelings I Struggle To Put Into Words.

In Your Presence, My Emotions Swirl, Leaving Me Both Speechless And Spellbound. My Love For You Is Profound, An Unending Journey That I Am Grateful To Embark Upon. You Are The Melody To My Heart's Song, And Even In Silence, I Hope You Feel The Depth Of My Adoration."

99. FIRST GIRL

"You Are The First Girl,
Even Whose Betrayal I Yearn For,
Just The Sight Of You Makes My Heart Race,
A Feeling That I Can't Ignore.

When I See You, Petals Bloom On My Heart's Empty
Branch,
Your Presence Awakens Every Season Of My Desire,
You Turn The Sun's Rays Into Clouds,
And The Moonlight Goes Wild, Caught In Your Fire.

You Make The Fairies Glide Over Tranquil Lakes,
As If They've Lost Their Wits In Your Charm,
The Waves, Once Still, Come Alive,
Echoing The Magic Of Your Calm.

Every Love Story Seems Real When You Are Near,
The World Becomes Beautiful, And My Worries
Disappear,
You Are The First Girl Who Fills My Soul With Bliss,
In Your Gaze, I Find A Perfect Kind Of Peace And
Happiness.

Every Moment Spent With You Feels Like A Treasure,
A Universe Unfolds, Rich In Love's Sweet Measure.
You Are Not Just A Girl; You Are My Dream Come True,
Forever And Always, My Heart Belongs To You.
You Are That First Girl"

100. CALLED

"I Held My Silence, Knowing Well The Cost,
For Those Who Wander Rarely Return When Called.
In My Heart, A Longing Softly Embossed,
Yet Their Echoes Fade, Leaving Me Enthralled.

In The Stillness, Where Whispers Intertwine,
I Wait For Your Presence, A Love Undefined.
Every Moment, I Cherish, Every Sigh,
Wishing You'd Hear My Heart's Quiet Cry.

Though Distance May Keep Us Worlds Apart,
Your Name Is The Melody That Lingers In My Heart.
I Call Out To You In The Night's Gentle Breeze,
Hoping You'll Return, With My Soul At Ease.

But If The Shadows Of Doubt Ever Creep,
Know That My Love Is A Promise I Keep.
For Every Silence Speaks Volumes Of Care,
In The Depths Of My Being, I Know You Are There."

101.BROKEN HEARTS

"They Never Flourish Again, Those Hearts
Once Scattered, Never To Be Whole Again,
No Matter How Beautifully The Grave Is Adorned,
The Dead Remain Silent, Their Warmth Forever Mourned.

In The Realm Of Love, Where Our Souls Intertwine,
I Find Myself Reflecting On What Was Once Divine.
Hearts, Once Vibrant, Can Be Torn Apart,
Leaving Echoes Of Laughter That Now Break My Heart.

Oh, My Beloved, You Are The Essence Of My Dreams,
Yet I Fear That Love, Once Lost, Is Not What It Seems.
For Every Moment Shared, A Memory That Glows,
But Like A Fleeting Shadow, It Fades And Then Goes.

No Embellishment Can Bring Back What's Lost,
In The Depth Of My Longing, I Bear The Cost.
Even The Brightest Flowers Wilt In Time's Cruel
Embrace,
Leaving Behind A Longing, A Void That None Can
Replace.

So Let Us Cherish Each Heartbeat, Each Glance,
For The Beauty Of Love Is Found In Every Chance.
Hold Me Close, As The Night Whispers Soft And Low,
For Once Hearts Are Shattered, They Rarely Will Grow.

Let Our Love Be The Light That Defies All Despair,
In This Fragile Existence, Let Us Nurture With Care.
For I Would Rather Feel The Warmth Of Your Hand,
Than Live In A World Where Our Hearts Cannot Stand."

102. BESEECH

"My Dove, I Beseech The Heavens Above,
Do Not Let God Keep You Far From My Heart.
In Every Moment Without You, I Ache,
Longing For The Spark That We Once Shared, Now Apart.

May God Grant Us The Strength To Bridge This Distance,
To Face The World's Trials Together Once More.
When You Were Near, My Heart Danced With Joy,
But Now It Trembles, Echoing A Love That's Sore.

Tell The Universe That My Eyes Yearn For You,
They Flutter With Hope At The Thought Of Your Embrace.
If You Must Smile, Know It Brings Both Joy And Pain,
A Bittersweet Reminder Of The Love We Chase.

I Wish You Could See How Deep My Feelings Run,
How Every Heartbeat Whispers Your Name In The Night.
Come Back To Me, Love, And Understand This Truth:
In Your Absence, I'm Lost; With You, Everything Feels
Right."

They Say Life Is Hard:

"Do You Fear Life?
Life Is Something You Are, And Life Is Something I Am
Too.

Do You Fear People?
A Person Is Something You Are, And A Person Is
Something I Am Too.
A Person Has A Voice And A Story;
You Do Not Fear Them,

But Do You Fear The Unsaid?
Do You Fear The Moments That Have Not Yet Arrived?
Do You Fear The Very Arrival Of Those Moments?
You've Already Experienced The Era Of Darkness,
Yet You Still Believe In Desires And Dreams.

This Night Of Silence Is A Path To The Divine,
But What Do You Truly Understand?
If The Lips Don't Move, The Hands Rise,
The Hands Rise To Become The Signs Of The Path, To
Become The Voice Of Light, To Rise As The Morning's
Call.

Do You Fear The Light?
You Are Light, And I Am Light Too.
On The City's Horizons,

The Shadow Of The Divine Has Been Purified At Last.
The Cloak Of The Night Has Been Torn Apart; It Has
Turned To Dust At Last.
From The Depths Of Humanity, A Song Of Freedom Has
Emerged,

A Call Of Essence Has Resonated.
On The Path Of Longing, As If The Travelers Have Been
Gripped By A New Fervour,
A New Passion Has Seized Man;
Look, Man Smiles, See The City Flourishing Again.

Do You Still Fear?
Yes, You Are Here, And Yes, I Am Here Too.
Do You Still Fear?

"My Dove,

Do You Fear Life? It's A Profound Journey We Are Both On, One That Shapes Us In Ways We May Not Yet Understand. Life Is A Canvas We Paint Together, Filled With Colours Of Joy, Sorrow, And Everything In Between.

Do You Fear Man? You And I Are Both Human, Capable Of Kindness, Strength, And Vulnerability. Yet, We Often Hide From The Truth Of Our Existence. A Man Is Not Just A Being; He Is A Voice, A Storyteller Of His Own Experiences. But You Need Not Fear Him, For In Him Lies A Part Of You.

What About The Things Left Unsaid? Do You Find Yourself Trembling At The Thought Of Moments Yet To Arrive? Those Very Moments That Hold Our Future, The Dreams We Long For? We've Both Traversed The Shadows Of Uncertainty And Fear, Yet Here We Are, Still Believing In Our Desires, Still Yearning For More.

The Silence Of The Night Can Be Daunting, Yet It Is Also A Pathway To Something Divine. It's In This Quiet That We Often Discover Who We Truly Are. If Our Words Fail, Let Our Hands Speak Instead, Guiding Us Toward Clarity, Lighting Our Path With The Warmth Of Hope.

Do You Fear The Light? Remember, We Are Both Light. We Bring Warmth To Each Other's Lives. The Shadows That Once Loomed Large Have Finally Receded. The Darkness Has Transformed Into Dust, Leaving Us Free To Embrace The Brilliance Of What Lies Ahead.

From The Depths Of Our Humanity, A Song Of Freedom Emerges—An Anthem Of Our Shared Essence. As We Walk The Path Of Our Desires, Let Us Find That New Fervour Together, Igniting A Passion That Will Sustain Us.

Look Around, My Love. See How We Flourish Together. Do You Still Fear? Yes, We Are Here, In This Moment, Alive And Vibrant. Let Go Of That Fear, For Together We Can Face Anything That Comes Our Way.

Do You Still Fear? I Am Here For You, And I Will Always Be."

103. DIMMING EVENING

*"When The Dimming Evening Of Memories Falls,
I Catch A Glimpse Of A Moment,
An Echo Of Your Love, So Profound,
A Final Heartbeat, A Whisper Of What Was.*

*The Pain Within Me Surged,
So Deep, I Wished To Escape Its Grasp,
I Yearned For The Relief It Promised,
Yet My Heart Resisted, Unwilling To Linger.*

*In The Twilight Of Our Shared Dreams,
Every Breath Carries Your Name,
Each Sigh A Reminder Of What We Had,
A Bittersweet Symphony Of Love And Loss.*

*How Could I Let Go Of The Warmth We Shared?
Even As The Shadows Grew Long,
My Soul Clung To The Light Of Your Laughter,
The Way Your Eyes Danced With Joy.*

*I Wanted To Chase Away The Ache,
But The Thought Of You Held Me Captive,
And Though I Sought To Move On,
My Heart Remains Tethered To Your Essence.*

*In Every Moment Of Solitude,
I Feel The Weight Of Your Absence,
Yet I Cherish The Traces You Left,
In Every Heartbeat, Every Tear."*

"In Every Dawn, I See Reflections Of You,

In The Gentle Light, In The Sky's Deep Hue.

The Seasons Change, Yet My Heart Remains Still,

In The Quiet Moments, It's Your Presence I Feel.

The Streets We Once Walked Whisper Tales Of The Past,

Memories Of Laughter, Moments That Couldn't Last.

I Find Solace In Shadows, Where Your Essence Resides,

Yet With Each Passing Day, It's Your Absence That Divides.

So Here I Am, Yearning Beneath The Moon's Glow,

Caught In A Dream Where Only Your Love Can Flow.

Life Unveils Its Secrets, And I'm Left To Decipher,

Every Heartbeat Echoes, My Longing Only Grows Richer.

What's Left Of This Home Without Your Warm Embrace?

Each Little Thing Shattered, A Reminder Of Your Grace.

Yet In The Pain Of Loss, I Still Find A Spark,

For In My Heart's Chamber, You'll Never Depart."

104. FADED TIES

"My Dove, It Feels As If Time Has Stood Still,
Each Memory Of You A Soft Whisper In The Dark.
When All Ties Have Faded,
Your Essence Still Warms My Soul.
I Often Wonder, Am I Truly Alive,
Or Do You Still Exist Within Me?

In Those Fleeting Moments,
When We Laughed And Shared Our Dreams,
You Were My Universe,
And I Was Simply Lost In Your Light.

Though The World Outside Feels Barren,
With Souls Wandering Aimlessly,
I Search For The Magic We Once Had,
And Yearn For The Connection That Still Lingers.

The City Is Filled With Shadows,
But Your Memory Shines Brightly,
Guiding Me Through The Labyrinth Of Longing,
Reminding Me That Love, True Love, Never Truly Fades.

So Tell Me, In This Vast Silence,
Do You Still Feel Me?
In This Intricate Dance Of Life,
Is There Still A Place For Us?

Let's Rewrite Our Story,
For The Flame That Ignited Our Hearts,
Is Not Extinguished But Merely Waiting,
To Burst Forth Anew, In All Its Brilliance."

My Heart's Offering;

I Have Filled My Lap With Thorns,
So That Every Branch Of The Flower Blooms,
In The Hope That Beauty Can Ease The Pain,
And Cleanse Your Embrace Of All Impurities,
In The Tender Gardens Of Our Shared Memories.

In My Longing, I Find Myself Defeated,
For I Wish Only To See The Joy In Your Eyes Once More.
Each Fleeting Moment, Like Morning Dew,
Reflects The Essence Of A Rose I Cannot Touch,
As I Slither Through The Silence Of My Heart,
Winding Through The Shadows Of Your Absence.

In A Flash, I Dance Alone In Moonlight,
Searching For Your Laughter In The Stars,
While The Sun's Warm Embrace Feels Cold Without You.
I Wander Lost In The Melodies Of Life,
Yearning For That Moment When We Were Whole,
When Your Love Was The Anchor Of My Soul.

Then, In A Sudden Spark Of Memory,
I Peek Through The Veil Of Lightning,
Hiding In The Depths Of Blue,
While Arrows Of Regret Fly Through Time,
My Face Veiled In Shadows Of What Once Was.

*Ah! How Fleeting And Uncertain These Moments Of Life
Are,
Yet, Among Them, Some Persist,
Living On In The Heartbeat Of My Love For You.
Every Beat Echoes Your Name,
Every Whisper Of The Wind Carries Your Essence,
For You Are The Heart Of My Existence,
The Joy That Colours My World.*

*But Now, Without You, Everything Feels Muted,
A Canvas Lacking The Vibrance Of Your Laughter,
An Empty Garden Where Flowers Once Bloomed.
I Long For Your Return, To Fill My Life Again,
To Rewrite The Verses Of Our Love Story,
To Bask In The Light Of Your Smile.*

*I Reach Out Across The Silence,
Hoping You Can Hear The Cries Of My Heart.
Come Back To Me, My Love,
For In Your Absence, I Am But A Shadow,
Waiting For The Sun Of Your Presence
To Illuminate My World Once More."*

105. TRUE LOVE?

"If My Lips Could Speak The Depth Of Love,

I Would Show You What True Love Is Made Of.

How I'd Hold You Close, So No One Else Could Claim,

If I Were Yours, I'd Reveal Love's Very Name.

I Wish I Could Teach You Through My Every Sigh,

To Understand The Meaning Behind Every Cry.

Oh, How I Long For You To Ask, To Inquire,

What Love Truly Is, Igniting The Fire.

In Each Heartbeat, In Every Silent Tear,

Lies A Story Of Longing, Of Holding You Near.

You, Who Once Held My Heart In Your Gentle Hand,

If You'd Just Return, I'd Help You Understand.

Let Me Show You The Colours Of Love's Embrace,

In Every Moment Shared, In Every Trace.

For You Are The Muse That Ignites My Soul,

Without You, My Love, I Am Not Whole.

With Open Arms, I Await Your Return,

Wishing You'd See The Love I Can't Hide.

Come Back To Me, Let's Rewrite Our Tale,

For In Your Absence, I Have Grown Pale."

In The Shadows Of Love;
*I Shall Not Gaze Upon The Path Of Death, For It Brings
No Solace Without You Near,
Longing For Your Presence, Yet If You Choose To Stay
Away, I Cannot Call You Here.*

*The Sorrow Of My Heart Speaks, Yet Finds No Words To
Convey,
What Can One Say In This World, Where Words Fail To
Hold Their Sway?*

*I Call Out To You, Oh Spirit Of My Heart,
But Let It Be Such That You Come To Me, And Never Part.*

*Others Wander, Holding Onto Your Letter,
If Asked About It, They Hide It, Feeling It's A Treasure.*

*What Can Be Said Of The Games We Played, The Passion
That Thrived?
The Veil Was Lifted, Yet The Truth Remains Uncontrived.*

*I Shall Not Look Upon The Path Of Death, For It Brings
No Solace Without You Near,
Longing For Your Presence, Yet If You Choose To Stay
Away, I Cannot Call You Here.*

Love Cannot Be Forced! It's That Flame Of Yearning,
That Ignites Yet Cannot Be Tamed, Leaving My Heart
Burning.

Come Back To Me, My Love, Let The Stars Align,
For In This Dance Of Hearts, Your Soul Must Intertwine."

106. YOUR GAZE

"You Never Asked For Grand Displays,

Yet Here I Stand, Lost In Your Gaze.

A Thousand Thoughts Swirl In My Mind,

A Connection So Rare, It's Hard To Find.

You've Woven Into My Every Day,

A Quiet Presence, A Gentle Sway.

Though Words May Tremble On My Lips,

I Carry You In Every Heartbeat's Rhythm.

I Wish To Share My Heart In Silence,

In Moments Where Love Finds Its Balance.

Even If Unspoken, Know This Is True:

In Every Glance, My World Revolves Around You.

Your Laughter Dances Like The Light,

A Melody That Makes Everything Right.

Though I May Not Voice What I Feel,

My Heart Holds A Truth That's So Very Real.

You Once Said, "Don't Speak Of This,"

But How Can I Hide Such A Bliss?

In Dreams And Shadows, You Reside,

A Beautiful Secret I Cannot Abide.

Let's Tread This Path Without A Map,

In Shared Smiles And Gentle Gaps.

No Need For Words That Bind Or Confine,

Just Know, My Dear, You Are Forever Mine."

107. CAST DOUBT UPON ME

"Who Has Cast Doubt Upon Me,
In My Red Shawls, Who Has Poured This Blue Poison?
Why Has This Season Turned So Unkind,
Where The Rain No Longer Soaks My Clothes,
And The Paths Refuse To Speak To Me Openly?
Why Do The Silences No Longer Share Their Secrets,
Whispering Truths They Once Confided In Me?

Just Days Ago, The Rain Used To Drench My Attire,
The Seasons Were Gentle, Embracing Me Warmly,
And The Roads Would Welcome Me With Open Arms,
While The Stillness Would Unveil Its Heart's Mysteries.
Only Days Ago, In The Embrace Of Nature,
We Shared A Bond With The Rains, The Roads,
And The Silences, Weaving Our Connection Deep.

But Now, Everywhere I Turn,
Strange Walls Of Unfamiliarity Rise,
Echoing The Loneliness Of Unkind Moments.
A Whisper Of Despair Fills The Air,
Who Has Turned My Vibrant Red Shawls To Shades Of
Blue?
Who Has Injected This Poison Into My Veins?
Who Has Cast Doubt Upon Me?

My Heart Aches For The Warmth We Once Shared,
The Laughter That Danced Like Sunlight Between Us,
The Moments That Felt Like Eternity In Your Presence.
I Long For The Days When The World Felt Alive,
When Each Raindrop Was A Note In Our Song,
And Each Path Led Me Closer To Love's Embrace.
Now, I Search For The Joy We Once Held,
Wishing For The Touch Of Your Hand,
The Sound Of Your Laughter That Once Filled The Air.

Come Back, My Love, Let Us Reignite The Spark,
Let The Rains Soak Me Anew,
Let The Seasons Wrap Me In Their Warmth.
Let The Paths Speak To Me Again,
And The Silences Share Their Secrets.
Together, Let's Break Down These Walls,
And Cast Away The Shadows Of Doubt.
For In Your Presence, I Find My Solace,
In Your Love, I Rediscover My Home."

108. MY WARDROBE

"There's No Pretence In This Bond We Share,

For You To Keep The Truth At Bay, It's Rare.

If You Choose To Keep Us In The Dark,

Then Let Your Silence Be Our Guiding Spark.

But How Wonderful It Would Be, My Dear,

If Together We Could Face The World, Without Fear.

How Nice It Would Be If We Lived Together,

*Your Clothes Would Fill My Wardrobe, Our Shared Space
A Tether.*

A Tapestry Of Moments, Woven With Light.

We Can Unravel Easily, That's True,

But There's A Puzzle Only We Can Construe.

Your Essence Shines Just Above The Mundane,

Our Love, A Dance That Can't Be Contained.

The Storyteller Has Penned Our Roles With Care,

Not Just Actors, But A Love That's Rare.

We Drift Through Days, Longing To Stay,

Yet In This Vastness, We Find Our Way.

No One Else Can Match The Depth We See,

In The Quiet Of The Night, It's You And Me.

Though The World May Not Understand Our Song,

In Our Hearts, We Know Where We Belong."

109. VISION OF BEAUTY

" You Seem To Move Even In The Picture,

As If You've Just Left My Heart, Still Ablaze With Your Name.

Every Season Feels Like A Dance When You're By My Side,

In June's Warm Sunshine, Like The Monsoon's Gentle Tide.

Your Essence Lingers, A Fragrance So Divine,

Like The Folds Of A Dupatta, Wrapped In Love's Design.

You Carry The Elegance Of A Palace So Grand,

A Vision Of Beauty, Forever At My Command.

With Each Glance, My Heart Races, A Symphony Of Delight,

In The Quiet Of The Night, You Are My Guiding Light.

Every Moment Shared Is A Treasure, Pure And True,

In The Canvas Of My Life, It's Only Painted With You.

Your Laughter, Like Music, Fills The Air With Cheer,

In Every Whispered Promise, I Hold You So Near.

Together We Weave Dreams, Like Stars In The Sky,

You Are My Forever, My Love, My Reason Why."

110. SOLITUDE

"My Dove, How Long Must I Endure This Solitude?
Each Day Feels Heavier, Each Moment A Struggle.
I Find Myself Longing For A Light To Break Through This
Darkness,
Someone To Lift The Shadows From My Heart,
To Shower Me With Comfort And Love.

I Yearn For The Day When Someone Might Argue For My
Heart,
To Passionately Return From Their Own Journey, To
Breathe Warmth Into My Cold Existence,
And Place Their Hands Upon My Aching Soul,
Reminding Me That I Am Not Alone.

I Dream Of Soft Whispers, Tender Confessions,
Words That Acknowledge The Burdens I Carry,
A Recognition Of The Silent Battles I Fight Each Day,
A Gentle Reassurance That I Am Seen,
That My Pain Has Not Gone Unnoticed.

In Your Embrace, I Seek Solace;
In Your Presence, I Long To Feel Alive Again.
So, My Love, Let Us Break These Chains Of Solitude
Together,
For With You, I Believe I Can Endure Anything.
You Are The Light I've Been Searching For,
The Reason I Can Hope, The Strength To Carry On."

111. MY WORLD

"My Dove, The Moment I Laid My Eyes On You, Everything Changed. I Understood That Within A Single Person Lies A Universe Of Emotions, Dreams, And Possibilities.

You Are Not Just A Part Of My Life; You Are My World. Your Laughter Fills My Heart With Joy, And Your Presence Brings A Sense Of Completeness I Never Knew I Was Missing. In You, I See Beauty, Strength, And A Love That Encompasses Everything I Hold Dear. You Are My Inspiration, My Solace, And My Everything.

With You, I Feel As Though The Vastness Of Existence Is Captured In A Single Glance, A Simple Touch, And A Shared Moment. When I Saw You, I Realized That One Person Can Embody The Entire World. Truly, You Are My World."

112. OUR CONNECTION

*"Now Our Connection Is No More
Now, I No Longer Hold A Place In Your Heart,
You Don't Come To Me In Dreams Anymore.
The Days We Cherished In Love Have Passed,
I Hold No Intent For Hatred, That I'm Sure.*

*I Will Forget You One Day, Perhaps-
That's A Hope I Cling To, But Not A Promise.
If Time Allows, We May Meet Again,
But You Seem Indifferent, And I Won't Impose.*

*Once, Your Laughter Filled My Days With Light,
Every Moment With You Felt So Right.
Yet Now, It Seems My Feelings Weigh Me Down,
While You Carry On, With A Distant Frown.*

*I Won't Burden You With What's In My Heart,
You've Moved On, While I Stand Apart.
Though I Cherish The Memories We Once Shared,
I'll Keep My Silence, Knowing You've Not Cared.*

*So Here's To You, The Love I Once Knew,
The Moments We Laughed, The Dreams That Felt True.
Though My Heart Still Feels, I'll Remain Discreet,
Wishing You Well, From A Distance, Bittersweet."*

113. BLAME

*"I Never Let Any Blame Fall On You
In A Poem, I Kept Your Name From Surfacing,
You Called Me A Failure One Day, Yet I Remained,
I Never Let Myself Be Of Any Use To Anyone,
Not Even To My Own Heart, Which You Once Claimed.*

*Not A Single Memory Forgotten,
Each Scar Still Throbs With Pain Unspoken,
I Guarded Our Moments, Holding Tight To Each Trace,
Never Allowing Solace To Take Over, Feeling Broken.*

*In Shadows Of Longing, Your Laughter Still Lingers,
Every Whispered Promise Haunts Me Through The Night,
You Were My Dawn, My Dream Woven With Silver,
Now, I Chase Echoes, Lost Without Your Light.*

*Every Tear That Falls Is A Testament To My Love,
Each Day Without You, A Reminder Of Your Grace,
I Wish To Turn Back Time, To Hold You Close Once More,
To Mend The Pieces And Rekindle The Warm Embrace.*

*Though You've Walked Away, I'll Keep Your Essence Near,
For Love Knows No Boundaries, It Transcends All Space,
Come Back, Dear Heart, Let's Write A New Chapter,
Together, Let's Turn The Pages, Restoring Our Place."*

114. MISUNDERSTANDING

"It Hurts To Reflect On How Misunderstandings Drove Us Apart. You Walked Away, Leaving Me In A Place Filled With Unspoken Words And Unanswered Questions. You Had No Trust In Me, And I Had No Hold Over Your Heart, Yet Here I Remain, Exactly Where You Left Me.

When Commitment Falters, The Pain Of Separation Can Feel Insurmountable. I Often Wonder How We Reached This Point. What Sorrow Could Have Been Avoided Had We Understood Each Other Better?

I Chose To Stay, Lingering In The Memories We Built Together. While You Moved On With A Smile, I Stand Still, Hoping That One Day We Might Bridge The Gap That Misunderstanding Created. The Laughter We Shared Echoes In My Heart, A Bittersweet Reminder Of What We Had.

Despite The Distance, A Part Of Me Still Holds Onto Hope. Perhaps One Day, Our Paths Will Cross Again, And We Can Find The Clarity We Once Lacked. Until Then, I Remain Here, Waiting And Remembering."

115. STONE HEART

"My Dove, When I Think Of You, It's Like The Most Delicate Fragrance Drifting Through The Air, Tantalizing And Ephemeral.

I Once Felt Alive, Vibrant With Emotion, Sharing Beauty With The World, Like Distributing Flowers To Brighten The Lives Of Others.

But In This Act Of Giving, I Realize I Have Become Hardened, Like Stone-My Heart Encased In A Shell.

Without You, Those Moments Lose Their Colour, And I Long For The Warmth Of Your Presence To Awaken My Soul Once More.

You Are The Essence I Seek, The One Who Can Transform My Stone Heart Back Into A Blooming Garden."

116. ONE GIRL

"In A Moment, I Have Seen Centuries,
In One Girl, I Have Seen The World.
She Is Not The One Who Left Me,
She Is The One Who Has Seen My Flaws."

In The Briefest Moments We Shared, I Felt As Though I Had Experienced Lifetimes. Each Second With You Was Rich With Meaning, And Every Glance Felt Eternal. Though You Are No Longer By My Side, The World I Saw In You Remains Vivid In My Heart.

You Left Me Due To Misunderstandings, Yet My Love For You Has Not Faded. You Were Never Like Those Who Turned Away When Faced With Imperfections. You Embraced My Flaws, Understanding That They Are Part Of Who I Am.

You Saw Beyond The Surface, Recognizing The Depth Of My Soul. Your Acceptance Made Me Feel Cherished, Even In My Moments Of Weakness.

Though You Have Departed, The Impact You Made On My Life Is Indelible. You Opened My Eyes To A World I Never Knew Existed, Transforming Ordinary Moments Into Cherished Memories. Your Love Showed Me The Beauty Of Vulnerability And The Strength Found In Being Truly Seen.

I Carry With Me The Lessons You Taught Me And The Dreams We Shared. I Want You To Know That I Will Wait Forever For You To Be Mine Again. Even In Your Absence, I Hold You Close In My Heart, Forever Grateful For The Time We Had."

117. LOVE'S TRUE COST

"Ask Me What Love's True Cost Is,

Ask Me What Love Has Truly Lost,

When Even In Giving My All, I Face The Frost.

A Life Spent In Loyalty, Year After Year,

Yet You Say I'm Foolish, My Heart Unclear.

With Every Breath, I've Whispered Your Name,

But You See Only Shadows, Not The Heart's Flame.

I've Worn My Heart On My Sleeve So Wide,

Yet You Question My Sanity, Dismiss My Pride.

I've Sacrificed Dreams, And Moments That Shine,

But To You, They Seem Trivial—What's Yours Is Mine.

An Age Devoted, Through Laughter And Tears,

Still, You Wonder Why I'm Lost In My Fears.

In The Silence, My Heart Still Calls Out For You,

Each Beat, A Reminder Of Love That Is True.

Yet You Turn Away, Blind To The Spark,

While I Stand Here Waiting, Lost In The Dark.

So Ask Me What Love's Real Pain Can Be,

When You Hold My Heart, Yet Don't Truly See.

I'm Just A Soul Yearning For Your Embrace,

Hoping One Day, You'll Recognize My Grace."

118. THIS ERA

"May This Era Be Blessed For You,

May This Era Bring You Joy,

Far From The Sorrows We Once Shared,

You, Who Shattered My Tender Heart,

Now, At Ease, You Walk Away, Unaware.

You Bled The Essence Of A Future Bright,

In Fragrant Dreams That Felt So Right.

Did You Cherish My Love, Or Let It Fade,

Leaving Me In Shadows, Lost And Betrayed?

Now, I Wander Through Echoes Of Our Past,

Haunted By Dreams That Couldn't Last.

Every Whispered Promise, Every Soft Glance,

Fades Into Silence, A Lost Romance.

The Pain Lingers Like An Unhealed Scar,

A Reminder Of Love That Wandered Too Far.

In Your Absence, I Find Only Despair,

Yearning For The Warmth Of The Love We Shared.

As You Flourish In Your Newfound Grace,

I'm Left Here, With Memories I Can't Erase.

If Only You'd Seen The Depths Of My Care,

Maybe Then You'd Realize What We Could've Shared.

But Now, I Stand Amidst The Ruins Of Hope,

A Heart That Longs, Struggling To Cope.

With Each Passing Day, I Learn To Endure,

Yet The Ache Of Your Absence Remains So Pure.

May Your Days Be Bright, May You Find Your Way,

Though You May Not Feel The Love I Still Portray.

In This Silence, I'll Cherish What Was Once Ours,

Even As I Watch You Dance Among The Stars."

119. UNDER THE SAME SKY

"When The Moon Is Half And Distant,

When The Moon Hangs Low And Shadows Play,

Do You Ever Sigh And Think Of Our Days?

Though You Might Not Dwell On What We Used To Share,

I Know In Quiet Moments, My Memory Finds You There.

In Bustling Gatherings, You Wear A Smile,

Yet I Wonder If My Absence Lingers For A While.

Do You Steal A Glance At The Stars Above,

And Feel A Flicker Of The Warmth Of Our Love?

The Hours Stretch Long As You Laugh And Dance,

But In The Silence Of Night, Do You Give Our Past A Chance?

ME IN YOUR LONGING

As Darkness Envelops, Do You Recall Our Dreams,

In The Stillness, Are You Haunted By Those Beams?

Don't Think I'm Alone In The Depths Of Night,

My Heart Whispers Your Name In The Fading Light.

Every Sigh I Take, Every Breath I Find,

Is A Testament To The Love That Still Binds.

So When The Moonlight Bathes You In Its Glow,

Know That A Part Of Me Is With You, Though Far, Though Low.

And Though Life Moves On, And You Wear Your Grace,

I Hold Onto The Hope That You Still Find A Trace.

A Trace Of Us Lingering In The Depths Of Your Heart,

A Reminder That True Love Never Truly Departs.

So, In Those Quiet Moments When You Reflect And Sigh,

Remember I'm Here, Loving You From Afar, Under The Same Sky."

"Where Are You Now?

Where Are You Now, In This Moment So Still?

I Am Not Where You Are; Yet, Your Absence Is A Thrill.

You Haunt My Thoughts, Like Shadows At Night,

My Heart Aches For Your Presence, A Lingering Light.

Your Love Was A Remedy For My Weary Soul,

Now I Suffer Alone, You Were My Whole.

In The Silence Of Night, I Hear Your Name,

Each Memory A Spark, Igniting The Flame.

You Promised To Stand By Me Through The Pain,

Yet Now, I'm Left To Bear This Heart's Heavy Chain.

ME IN YOUR LONGING

What Did You Gain From This Love That We Shared?

Did You Find Solace, While I Was Left Bare?

Like Romeo's Tale Of Longing And Despair,

You Vanished From My Life, Leaving Just Air.

The World Moves On; You Find Joy And Delight,

While I Dwell In Shadows, Lost In The Night.

Oh, But Let Me Tell You This One Truth,

In My Heart, You Remain My Eternal Youth.

We Are Bound By A Love That Time Cannot Sever,

In Every Heartbeat, You Are My Forever.

The Essence Of Beauty, In All That You Are,

I Search For Your Spirit, My Guiding Star.

So, As You Carry On, In Your World So Bright,

Know That My Love For You Is An Endless Fight."

120. OUR BOND

"In The Realm Of Love, Truth Is A Treasure,

Yet, Here We Stand, Surrounded By Whispers And Doubts.

Every Glance, Every Silence, Carries A Weight,

But Still, I Wish You Could See Beyond The Veils.

Let Not The Tales Of The World Define Our Bond.

Trust In The Moments We've Shared, In The Laughter And
Tears.

For Every Doubt Cast Like A Stone,

Remember The Warmth Of My Embrace, The Truth In My
Heart.

If I Could, I'd Shield You From The Chaos,

Wrap You In The Certainty Of My Love.

Let Our Eyes Meet, And In That Gaze, Find Solace-A
World Where Only We Exist, Free From Fears.

So Believe In The Love We Nurture,

In The Whispers Of The Night, In The Light Of Dawn.

For If I Were In Your Place, I'd Choose To See,

The Unwavering Love That Blooms Eternally."

121. LOST WITHOUT YOU

"Wherever You Are At This Moment, I Find Myself Lost Without You, Feeling An Emptiness That Echoes In Every Corner Of My Heart. Today, The Memory Of You Weighs Heavily On Me, And The Longing Is Almost Unbearable.

I Miss You So Deeply, And The Ache Of Your Absence Is A Constant Reminder Of How Incomplete My Life Feels Without You.

You Were The Balm For My Soul, The One Who Could Heal My Wounds With Just A Smile. Oh, How I Suffer In Silence, Drowning In A Sea Of Nostalgia And Yearning For Your Love.

Each Beat Of My Heart Is Filled With Memories Of Us, And Every Sigh Carries The Pain Of Your Distance. Your Love Was My Sanctuary, And Now, Without You, I Feel Lost In A Storm Of Sorrow.

Those Who Have Walked Beside Me May Offer Their Friendship And Understanding, But They Cannot Grasp The Depth Of My Emotions. They Don't Hear The Silent Cries Of My Heart, The Desperate Whispers That Reach Out For You In The Quiet Of The Night.

I Need To Express Just One Thing: I Long To Revisit Our Past, To Confront The Beautiful Moments We Shared That Now Feel Like Fleeting Shadows.

What Have You Truly Gained By Stepping Away From The Love We Nurtured? I Yearn For The Chance To Look Into Your Eyes Once More, To Speak My Heart Openly, And To Show You How Deeply I Cherish You. Just Like Romeo, Who Was Consumed By Madness, I Find Myself Wandering Through This World, Caught Between Love And The Ache Of Separation, While You Remain A Distant Dream.

This Tale Of Love Is Not Just Ours; It Is Woven Into The Fabric Of Time Itself. Whether It Is You Or Me, We Are Bound By A Connection That Transcends Everything-An Unbreakable Bond That Neither Distance Nor Time Can Sever. We Are The Essence Of Beauty, A Creation Of Love That Deserves To Be Cherished.

Please Understand That I Am Still Here, Waiting And Hoping For The Day When You Might Return. The Memories Of Our Laughter, Our Shared Dreams, And The Warmth Of Your Presence Linger In My Heart. I Yearn For The Moment When We Can Create New Memories, When I Can Hold You Close And Feel Whole Again.

I Want You To Know The Depths Of My Love And The Profound Pain Your Absence Has Caused Me. I Am Here, Always Believing In Us, Hoping That You Will Find Your Way Back To Me."

When I Think of You;
"Why Do You Feel So Good To Me?
When I Find The Time, I'll Ponder Deeply.

What Is There In You To Behold?
When I Find The Time, I'll Consider It Fully.

In The Seasons, In Fragrances,
In The Gentle Breeze, The Moonlit Dusk,

And In The Stars Above-Who Compares To You?
When I Find The Time, I'll Reflect On This."

122. A MOMENT

"Not A Moment's Glance Do I Receive From Her,
Yet This Heart Craves More Than Mere Whispers.
It Longs For A Love That Knows No Bounds,
A Passion That In Silence Profoundly Resounds.

In The Quiet Hours, Her Memory Takes Flight,
Haunting My Thoughts, A Bittersweet Light.
Each Heartbeat Whispers Her Name In The Dark,
A Melody Echoing, Igniting A Spark.

Though Distance Divides Us, My Soul Feels Her Near,
In Dreams, She Dances, Erasing All Fear.
But Waking Brings Anguish, A Longing So Deep,
A Void That Engulfs Me, No Promises To Keep.

I Wander Through Shadows Where Our Laughter Once
Played,
Each Memory A Treasure, A Bittersweet Cascade.
The Warmth Of Her Smile, The Grace Of Her Touch,
Reminds Me Of Love That Has Meant So Much.

Yet Here I Remain, Caught In This Bind,
Wishing She'd See The Love That I Find.
For In Every Moment, My Heart Beats True,
Desiring A Future Where It's Me And You.

So I Stand In The Silence, With Hopes Intertwined,
Longing For A Moment When Our Hearts Align.
Though A Glance May Be Fleeting, My Love's Never Shy,
For In Every Breath, It's Her Name That I Sigh."

123. LAKE LIKE EYES

"I Used To Look Into Her Lake-Like Eyes,
As If Someone Were Seeing The Ocean For The First Time.

In Her Gaze, I Found A Vastness,
A Deep Reflection Like Tranquil Waters,
Where Every Glance Revealed Hidden Depths,
Each Moment Felt Like An Endless Journey.

Those Eyes Sparkled With Mysteries Untold,
Echoes Of Waves Crashing On Distant Shores,
They Held The Beauty Of Uncharted Realms,
Inviting Me To Explore, To Lose Myself In The Depths.

With Each Look, I Discovered A New Horizon,
As If The Skies Shifted And Opened Up Wide,
And I, A Wanderer Seeking The Sublime,
Became Lost In The Vastness Of Her Soul.

Her Laughter Danced Like Sunlight On The Sea,
Illuminating The Shadows, Bringing Warmth,
In Her Presence, I Felt Time Stand Still,
As If The Universe Conspired To Pause, Just For Us.

Those Eyes, A Refuge From The Chaos,
Whispered Secrets Of Dreams Yet To Unfold,
I Learned To Navigate The Currents Of Her Heart,
Finding Solace In The Tide Of Her Love.

To Look Into Her Eyes Was To Embark On An Adventure,
A Journey Through The Infinite, The Beautiful Unknown,
And In Every Fleeting Moment, I Cherished The Wonder,
For Her Gaze Was My Ocean, Vast And Ever Inviting."

124. RENOWNED

"This Pain Is Unique, As I'm Drifting Away from You,
This Sorrow Is Distinct, It's Pushing Me Further From
Myself.
In Your Absence, I Write New Verses,
It's Your Heartache That's Making Me Renowned."

My Dove,
"In The Depths Of My Soul, I Find A Vast Ocean,
A Boundless Expanse Where My Emotions Flow.

Each Tear That Falls Carries A World Of Dreams,
Yet When I Confront My Destiny, It Feels Fragile, Ready
To Break.

The Thought Of Our Love, So Profound And Intricate,
Makes Me Tremble At The Thought Of Its Revelation.

I Hold Back, Fearing The Weight Of My Confession,
For Love That Is Shared Can Also Be A Double-Edged
Sword.

What If My Feelings Are Not Mirrored In Your Heart?
The Fear Of Losing What We Had Is Paralyzing.

Yet, In The Quiet Moments Between Us,
I Feel The Potential Of Our Hearts Intertwining.

So Here I Stand, Caught Between Vulnerability And Hope,
Longing To Share The Truth That Keeps Me Awake At
Night.

For In My Eyes, You Are The Tide That Lifts My Spirit,
And Though I Fear What May Come, I Yearn For The
Chance,

To Show You That My Love Is Not Just A Whisper,
But A Symphony Waiting To Be Played,
If Only You Could Hear The Music In My Heart."

125. LONGING TO MEET YOU

"Every Time I Meet You,
There's A Longing In My Heart,
An Unfulfilled Desire,
A Wish That Won't Depart.

Even After You've Gone,
Your Scent Lingers Near,
I Whisper To The Shadows,
Sharing Secrets, Soft And Clear.

In The Silence Of The Night,
Your Presence Wraps Around Me,
Like A Delicate Embrace,
Filling Spaces Where You Used To Be.

Memories Dance Like Flickering Flames,
Each Moment, A Cherished Frame,
A Melody Of Laughter, A Sigh Of Regret,
In Every Heartbeat, Your Name Is Set.

Though Distance May Divide Us,
And Time May Lead Us Astray,
The Bond We Forged Is Timeless,
In My Heart, You'll Always Stay."

126. DESTINY

"In The Tapestry Of Time, Where Moments Weave,

I Search For The Whispers That Make My Heart Believe.

But Like Fleeting Shadows, They Slip Through My Hands,

Those Precious Encounters That Love Understands.

Your Presence Eludes Me, Like A Star In The Night,

A Glimmer Of Hope That Fades Out Of Sight.

Every Heartbeat Echoes A Longing Profound,

For A Love So Rare, Yet Never To Be Found.

Though The Universe Spins, And The Seasons May Change,

My Heart Holds A Flame That Feels Distant, Strange.

Like Milne's Verses, Where Dreams Intertwine,

I Yearn For A Love That Was Destined To Shine.

So Here I Stand, With Words From My Soul,

Hoping One Day, We'll Make Each Other Whole.

Until That Moment, I'll Cherish The Thought,

Of The Love That Was Whispered, But Never Caught."

127. DELAYED

"When It's Time To Speak My Heart,
To Honour A Promise Made,
When I Long To Hear Your Voice,
To Bring You Back Into My World,
I Always Find Myself Delayed.

When I Wish To Offer Help,
To Support You In Your Dreams,
On Winding Paths That Lead To You,
When I Seek To Meet Your Gaze,
I Always Find Myself Delayed.

In The Changing Seasons Of Life,
When I Want To Hold You Close,
To Remember Moments Shared,
To Forget The Pains We've Faced,
I Always Find Myself Delayed.

When I Wish To Shield You From Sorrow,
To Share A Truth That Needs To Be Told,
When I Yearn To Whisper Love's Embrace,
I Find Myself Lost In Time,
And Always Find Myself Delayed."

128. UNINTERRUPTED AND UNWAVERING

In This Journey Of Love, Where Every Moment Is A Treasure, I Often Stumble In My Attempts To Express How Deeply You Are Etched In My Heart. Each Time I Gather The Courage To Reach Out, The World Seems To Conspire Against Me, Creating Distances I Never Intended.

As The Seasons Change, My Love For You Only Grows Stronger. I Find Myself Reminiscing About Our Shared Laughter, The Warmth Of Your Presence, And The Simple Joy Of Being Together. Yet, In The Busyness Of Life, I Let Precious Moments Slip Away, Wishing I Could Pause Time To Hold You A Little Longer.

There Are Times When I Feel The Weight Of Unspoken Words, The Urgency To Protect You From Life's Harsh Realities. I Want To Be Your Shield, To Lift You From Despair, But Still, I Hesitate, Caught In The Web Of My Own Hesitations.

Know This, My Love: Every Delay In My Heart's Expression Is Merely A Testament To The Depth Of My Feelings. I Long To Bridge The Gaps, To Turn My Intentions Into Actions, And To Show You The Love That Words Can Scarcely Convey.

I Promise That I Will Find A Way To Overcome The Barriers That Hold Me Back. For You Deserve All Of Me, Uninterrupted And Unwavering. Together, Let's Weave Our Dreams Into Reality, For I Will No Longer Let Time Delay The Love I Wish To Share With You.

129. SPOKEN

*"If She Had Looked At Me With Anger, I Would Have
Spoken To Her,
If There Were Any Hope, I Would Have Found My Words
To Share.
It Wasn't So Hard To Converse With Someone, You See,
If Only Someone Had Reached Out, I Would Have Dared
To Care.*

*In The Silence, I Waited, Each Moment Stretching Long,
Yearning For A Glance, A Sign, A Soft Reply In Our Song.
The Distance Between Us, A Chasm I Couldn't Bridge,
Yet The Thought Of Her Smile Was A Light On The Ridge.*

*I Replay Our Moments, The Laughter We Once Shared,
Every Whispered Secret, Every Glance That Declared.
But Now, In This Silence, I Feel The Weight Of The Night,
Wishing For The Courage To Turn Darkness To Light.*

*If She Had Spoken First, Would It Have Changed Our
Fate?
Would The Echoes Of Our Hearts Harmonize Instead Of
Wait?
In Dreams, I Paint Her Picture, In Hues Of Love And Pain,
And Hope That One Day Soon, We'll Dance In The Rain.*

*Here I Stand, With Words That Linger On My Tongue,
A Love Unspoken, A Melody Unsung.
If Only Fate Would Whisper, If Only Time Would Bend,
I'd Find The Strength To Tell Her, She Is My Heart's True
Friend."*

130. PERISH IN YOUR ABSENCE

*"As They Departed, The Ties Faded,
Yet There Were So Many Connections That Should Have
Brought Them Back.
Better To Complain About The Darkness Of Night,
Than To Let Our Own Flicker Of Light Extinguish In
Silence.*

*How Easy It Would Have Been To Perish In Your Absence,
My Love,
Yet, It Took A Lifetime To Bear This Pain Of Separation.
If Only The Celebration Of Our Demise Could Have Been
Held,
We Would Have Danced Joyfully, Even Shackled By Fate.*

*Did They Know Of Her Loyalty, Or Was It Merely A
Shadow?
Yet, Dear, I Held My Promises With Such Grace,
While I, In My Heart, Endlessly Yearned For You,
Finding Solace In Memories, Even As They Fade Away."*

As I Sit Here Reflecting On The Time We Spent Together, I Can't Help But Feel The Weight Of Your Absence. Just As The Poem Speaks Of The Bonds That Should Have Brought Us Closer, I Realize That Our Connection Was Woven With Threads Of Love And Understanding That Are Too Precious To Let Slip Away.

Every Moment Apart Is A Reminder Of How Easy It Could Have Been To Simply Dissolve Into Sorrow. Yet, Instead, I Find Myself Holding On, Clinging To The Light Of Our Shared Memories.

The Darkness Of This Night Feels Far More Daunting Without You By My Side. I Wish I Could Ignite That Familiar Warmth We Once Shared, But It Seems My Heart Struggles To Keep That Flame Alive.

It's Funny How The Heart Works-How It Yearns For The One It Loves, Even When It Feels Lost In The Shadows. I Often Think About How, If We Could Celebrate Our Love Even In The Face Of Challenges, We Would Dance Freely, Unburdened By The Pain Of Separation. The Thought Of Us Celebrating Together, Even In Tough Times, Gives Me Hope.

There Are Questions I Ponder: Did You Know How Deeply You Were Cherished? Did You Feel The Weight Of My Loyalty As I Carried Your Love Within Me? I Realize Now That Our Love Demands To Be Nurtured, Not Left To Wither In Silence.

I Long For The Day When We Can Bridge This Gap Between Us. Let Us Reignite That Spark, Breathe Life Into Our Bond, And Remember What Made Us So Vibrant Together. I Believe We Can Create A New Chapter Filled With Laughter, Understanding, And Unwavering Support."

131. STILLNESS OF NIGHT

"I Sent My Message Even In The Stillness Of The Night,

In The Absence Of You, The Moon Stood Bright.

The Arrival Of Love Warmed The Alley Of Faith,

So I Placed A Single Lamp At The Evening's Wraith.

In The Thirst Of Longing, Pride Held My Heart Tight,

When You Turned Your Gaze, I Raised My Cup In Delight.

Your Eyes Spoke Volumes, Sweet Words Unconfined,

I Laid All My Verses At Your Feet, Intertwined.

Look At The Dreams That Were Once Mine To Weave,

And Behold The Wounds That My Heart Must Grieve.

I Laid Bare My Soul For All To Perceive,

Each Sigh A Testament, Each Whisper To Believe.

And How Many Loves Will It Take To Show,

That Mothers Named Their Children After You, You Know?

For In Every Heartbeat, In Every Sigh,

Your Name Lingers, As The Stars Fill The Sky."

132. INDIFFERENT ONE

"Why Did I Offer My Heart To The Indifferent One,
To The One Accustomed To Betrayal,
To The One Who Knows Not Loyalty's Embrace,
Who Fails To Understand The Depth Of Longing,
And Brings Forth Only Sorrow's Celebration.

This Torment Is A Cruel Refrain,
Echoed In A World That Whispers Her Name,
A Beauty Unkind, A Deceiver By Trade,
An Artist Of Pain, A Master Of Despair.

She, Who Knows Not Affection,
Who Cannot Fathom The Warmth Of Desire,
Who Dismisses Comfort As Mere Illusion,
And Does Not Recognize Solace As Truth.

Her Promises Remain Unfulfilled,
Every Word A Half-Hearted Attempt,
Day And Night Are Consumed By Thoughts Of Her,
Yet She Arrives Unbidden, Indifferent To My Pleas.

No Spark Ignites The Heart's Flame,
No Warmth Lingers To Soothe The Ache,
And Silence Becomes The Language Of Our Distance,
As She Turns Away, Never To Hear My Sighs.

What Use Is A Heart So Laden With Hope,
If Unreturned, It Becomes A Hollow Echo?
I Can Lay My Desires At Her Feet,
Yet All I Receive Are Vacant Stares.

Why Boast Of A Heart That Bears Such Weight,
If Love Remains Unreciprocated?
In The Shadows, I Dwell, Contemplating,
What Is Love If Not Met With Yearning Eyes

If She Turns Away, What Remains For Me?
A Solitary Path Of Silent Wishes,

Yet My Soul Clings To The Memory Of Her Grace,
Unbeknownst To Her, She Holds My Heart Captive."

"In Your Eyes,
I May Seem Lost, Unaware,
But In Truth, I Hold The Care.
In Your Gaze, I Find My Place,
In Every Glance, I See Your Face.

Though Distance Stretches, Time Moves Slow,
My Heart Still Whispers What You Should Know.
You Are The Thought That Fills My Mind,
A Love So Deep, It's Hard To Find.

Each Moment Without You Feels Like A Night,
A Longing For The Warmth Of Your Light.
I Walk Through Crowds, Yet Feel Alone,
Your Absence Makes This Heart A Stone.

Come Back To Me, Let Our Souls Entwine,
For In Your Presence, Everything's Divine.
Together, We'll Weave The Dreams We Share,
For In Your Love, I Find My Air.

Though I May Seem Like A Distant Star,
Know That My Heart Has Travelled Far.
To You, My Love, My Longing Call,
In Your Eyes, I Want To Lose It All."

133. IN YOUR ARMS

*"The Way You Gaze At Us, My Love, With Such Tender
Care,
One Day, I'll Find Myself Resting In Your Arms, Unaware.*

*In The Quiet Moments When The World Fades Away,
I See Your Eyes Lingering, Inviting Me To Stay.*

*Your Gaze, A Soft Caress, Wraps Around My Heart,
Reminding Me Of The Bond That Will Never Part.*

*Though Time May Stretch Like Shadows In The Night,
Every Thought Of You Brings Warmth And Light.*

*I Remember The Laughter, The Whispers Shared,
A Connection So Deep, It Felt Almost Rare.*

*Yet Here I Stand, Yearning For Your Touch,
Hoping You Can See How I've Missed You So Much.*

*In Dreams, We Dance Under A Starlit Sky,
And In Those Moments, I Wish You Could Fly.*

*I Know The Distance Has Made Us Feel Apart,
But Know This, Dear Love, You Still Own My Heart.*

If Only You Could See, If Only You Could Know,
That In Your Embrace, My True Self Can Show.

So Come Back To Me, Let Our Souls Intertwine,
Let's Rewrite Our Story, Make Everything Divine.

For I Believe In Us, In The Love We Once Knew,
And I Long For The Day When I'm Back Close To You."

134. UNCERTAINTY

"In This World Where Uncertainty Reigns,
I Find Myself Adrift In Sorrow's Chains.
Each Moment Without You Feels Like An Eternity,
Days Blend Together, Stripped Of Clarity.

I Wish To Know The Path That Leads You Back To Me,
To Grasp Your Hand Again, To Feel You Near, To See.
The Seasons Pass, Yet Your Absence Remains,
Like Winter's Chill That Seeps Into My Veins.

I Wonder, As I Gaze At The Stars Above,
If They Whisper Your Name, As I Whisper My Love.
Every Dawn Without You Is A Heartache Anew,
Each Sunset A Reminder Of What We Once Knew.

The World Around Me Is A Canvas Of Gray,
With Echoes Of Laughter That Have Drifted Away.
I Crave The Bloom Of Our Love In Full Flower,
Yearning For Your Presence, Every Minute, Every Hour.

Though Life Moves Forward, My Heart Lingers Still,
In The Hope That Fate Might Bend To My Will.
So I Call Out To The Winds, With All My Might,
To Bring You Back To Me, To Make Everything Right.

In The Poetry Of My Heart, You Are The Refrain,
A Melody Sweet, In Joy And In Pain.
Until The Day We Meet Again, I'll Wait,
For In Your Arms Is My Destined Fate."

135. DAWN

"This Bright Light Of Dawn,
This Night, Heavy With Longing,
Was The Wait For Something More, But Is This The Dawn
We Sought?
This Is Not The Dawn We Dreamed Of, The One We Hoped
To Find,
When We Set Out, Hand In Hand, Searching For Joy,
Under The Vast Sky, Where The Stars Seem To Lead Us,
There Must Be A Shore Where The Waves Of Our Silent
Sorrow Calm,
Somewhere, Our Hearts' Weary Boat Will Find Rest."

"In Every Dawn That Breaks, I Feel The Weight Of My Longing For You. Each Moment Apart Is Like A Night That Stretches Endlessly, Filled With Unspoken Dreams. This Light That Shines Before Me Is Not Just A Dawn; It's A Reminder Of The Warmth Of Your Presence.

I Remember The Times We Walked Together, Hand In Hand, Believing We Would Find Joy In Every Step. We Were Adventurers In A World Painted With Hope, Searching For A Love That Felt As Vast As The Stars Above. Yet, Here I Stand, Feeling The Void Where Your Laughter Once Filled The Air.

Though We Wander Through Shadows, Searching For That Perfect Shore Where Our Hearts Can Finally Rest, I Know That Our Journey Isn't In Vain. Each Wave That Crashes Against Our Dreams Carries Whispers Of Love, Urging Us To Keep Moving Forward, To Seek That Tranquil Place Where We Can Be Whole Again.

I Hold On To The Belief That Somewhere, Under The Same Sky, Our Paths Will Intertwine Once More. Until Then, My Heart Remains Steadfast, Waiting For The Moment We Will Share That Beautiful Dawn, Together."

"My Dove, In Every Quiet Moment, I Find Myself Reaching Out To You. Even In The Darkest Nights, I Whisper My Thoughts, Hoping They Drift To You Like A Gentle Breeze. Each Time I Think Of Our Shared Moments, I Remember How Your Presence Ignites My Spirit.

The Anticipation Of Your Return Warms Me, Much Like The Evening Sun That Chases Away The Shadows. Just As A Lamp Flickers In The Dusk, My Heart Glows With The Hope Of Your Love.

Longing Can Be Fierce, Yet I Carry My Pride Like A Shield, Ready To Raise My Cup In Celebration The Moment I See You Again. Your Gaze, A Silent Promise, Weaves Its Way Into My Soul, And I Find Solace In Surrendering My Words At Your Feet, Each One A Token Of My Devotion.

Every Dream I Dream Is Painted With Your Essence, While Every Wound I Bear Is A Reminder Of How Deeply I Feel. I Lay My Heart Bare, Inviting You To Witness The Beauty And Pain Of My Love, A Blend Of Joy And Sorrow Intertwined.

So Tell Me, How Many Times Must I Profess My Love? How Many Names Must Echo Through Time Before The World Recognizes What You Mean To Me? With Each Beat Of My Heart, With Every Thought That Crosses My Mind, I Realize That My Life Is Forever Linked To Yours, And Your Name Shall Forever Be My Greatest Melody."

136. OCEAN OF LOVE

*"In The Depths Of The Sea, Where The Waves Kiss The
Shore,
I See Our Love Shimmering, A Treasure To Explore.
Each Ripple Whispers Your Name, A Song So Divine,
In This Vast Expanse, I Yearn For You To Be Mine.*

*This Heart, A Vessel, Ready To Plunge Into The Deep,
With Every Beat, It Dreams Of The Promises We Keep.
For Destiny Has Etched Our Souls In The Stars Above,
In Every Storm And Calm, It's You I Truly Love.*

*As I Sail Through Life's Currents, With Hopes Held High,
I Wonder If You Feel It Too, A Longing That Won't Die.
Like The Tides That Pull Me Closer, Your Essence I
Crave,
Together, Let's Navigate This Wild, Wondrous Wave.*

*So Let Our Hearts Dive Deep, Where Secrets Lie Unfurled,
In The Ocean Of Our Love, Let's Create Our Own World.
With Each Breath, Let's Embrace The Magic That We
Find,
For In This Endless Sea, Our Souls Will Be Entwined.*

*In The Ebb And Flow Of Time, In Every Fleeting Glance,
I Believe In Our Journey, In Love's Eternal Dance.
This Heart Will Find Its Harbour, Where It Truly Belongs,
In The Ocean Of Your Heart, Where Forever Sings Our
Songs."*

137. NOT AT ALL

"What Is This Sorrow? Is It Just The Heart's Habit?
Or Is There A Complaint Against Someone? Not At All.
It Is A Dream Without Fulfilment,
To Forget Is An Intention, Not At All.

Living Without Someone, Or Living With Their Memory,
It Takes Courage To Survive, Not At All.
In Any Form, My Heart Finds No Comfort!
For A Few Days, This Has Been My Condition, Not At All.

The One Who Holds You Without Holding You Anywhere,
That Is A Personal Kind Of Madness, Not At All.
Everyone Is Astonished By Your State,
You Are Also Surprised By This, Not At All.

We Are Not In Harmony With The World,
You Regret This, Not At All.
Was This What Was Destined?
This Is The Entire Narrative, Not At All.

The Painful Hopes You Have For Peace,
You Long For Safety, Not At All.
You Remain Lost In Thoughts And Dreams,

The Reason For This Is Free Time, Not At All.

I Have So Much Love For Those Far Away,
And Hatred For Those Close, Not At All.
The Reason For This Separation,
Is More Beautiful Than Me, Not At All."

138. SEARCH FOR

"What Folly It Is To Build A Home Upon The Sun,
Seeking Shade Where Warmth Burns Bright, Love's Race
Not Yet Run.
Even When Standing Tall, My Feet Find Only Mire,
Yet My Heart Yearns For The Solace Of Your Sweet
Desire.

I Wander Through The Bustling Cities, Dreams In Tow,
Carrying Hopes Like Lanterns, Guiding Me As I Go.
Amidst The Towering Structures That Pierce The Sky,
I Search For The Simplicity Of Our Shared Goodbye.

In The Noise Of Life, Where Bright Dreams Are Often
Spun,
I Long For The Quiet Comfort Found When Two Hearts
Are One.
For In Every Gleaming Facade, Every Radiant Light,
I See Only Reflections Of You, My Heart's Delight.

So Let Me Roam This Vibrant World, My Love As My
Guide,
To Find In Every Corner, The Warmth Where You Abide.
No Matter How Far I Wander, Or How High I Soar,
It Is Your Love I Treasure, Forever And Evermore."

139. HOME

"In The Shadows Of My Heart, Laughter Once Bloomed Bright,
But Time Has Silenced Its Melody, Shrouded It In Night.

Your Presence Was A Sunbeam, Warming Every Corner,
And Even Now, Without You, I Feel A Haunting Hunger.

You May Find A Shelter, A Space To Call Your Own,
But Know That In My Heart, There's Always Room Alone.

Its Walls Are Built Of Memories, Rich With Your Embrace,
A Sanctuary For Your Spirit, A Sacred, Cherished Place.

I Long For The Laughter We Once Shared In The Air,
Yet In Its Absence, Silence Wraps Me In Despair.

No Matter Where You Wander, Or Whom You Choose To See,
My Heart Will Always Cradle The Love You Gave To Me.

In The Quiet Of The Night, When Stars Begin To Weep,
I'll Hold Onto Our Moments, Through Shadows Dark And Deep.

*Though You May Seek A New Home, My Love Will Never
Fade,
For In My Heart, There's Always Room-A Love That Won't
Evade.*

*So If The World Should Change Us, And Time Pulls Us
Apart,
Remember, My Dear, You've Forever Claimed My Heart.*

*In Every Breath I Take, In Every Whispered Sigh,
You'll Always Have A Space Where Love Will Never Die."*

140. JUST FOR YOU

"These Tender Tones, Sweet Words, Are Just For You,

In This Gentle Speech, My Heart Feels True.

I Don't Share This Warmth With Anyone Else,

For In Your Presence, My Soul Truly Dwells.

In Every Whisper, In Each Soft Sigh,

I Find A Language That Soars, That Can Fly.

Your Laughter Dances, A Melody Sweet,

With Every Moment, My Heart Skips A Beat.

The World Fades Away When You Are Near,

In Your Eyes, I Find Solace, A World Crystal Clear,

With You, My Dove, I Share My Best,

In This Soft Language, I Feel So Blessed.

So Let These Words Wrap Around Your Heart,

A Love That's Unique A Beautiful Art,

For In Every Phrase And In Every Rhyme,

I Cherish You Deeply, Transcending All Time."

141. MY HEART'S GENTLE PLEA

" It's Enough That My Heart Has Found Its Way To You,

Even If Just For A Moment, A Glimpse Of Your View.

Where The Roads Were Meant To Stop,

Where I Should Have Turned, I've Lost That Thought.

What Matters Now Is The Joy Of Our Meeting,

Hold Onto This Moment, Its Warmth, Its Greeting.

Forget What Never Come To Be,

Let Go Of Dreams That Were Not Meant For Me.

The Rains Meant for Your Destiny,

Have Found Another's Roof To See.

Oh, Heed My Heart's Gentle Plea,

Forget The Past, Forget What Could Never Be.

In Every Whisper Of The Wind,

I Feel Your Essence Softly Pinned.

This Love, Though Fleeting, Is Deeply true,

In The Book Of My Heart, I Write For You.

As I Turn Each Page, I Find Your Name,

A Love That Burns, A Passionate Flame.

Let's Cherish The Moments That We Now Share,

For In Your Eyes, I Find My Prayer.

So, Here's To Us, To This Sweet Embrace,

To The Laughter, The Silence, The Tender Grace.

With Every Heartbeat, I Choose To Believe,

In The Beauty Of Love, And The Joy We Weave.

Forget What We Lost, Let The Past Fade Away,

In The Light Of Your Love, I Choose To Stay.

For In You, My Dove, I've Finally Found,

A Love That Is Timeless, A Bond That Is Profound."

142. ONE PERSON

" What Will They Give Me In This Trial,

When All I Bear Are Scars Of Denial?

Every Word I've Uttered Falls Flat,

What Significance Lies In My Statement,

Where's It At?

I Recognised My Solitude From The Crowd,

A Sense Of Detachment, So Pronounced, So Loud.

Why Don't They Speak In My Defence?

Words Vanish Into Silence, Leaving No Evidence.

If I Ever Meet You, There's One Thing To Ask:

Am I Still Safe In Your Heart, Or Have I Lost That Glow?

As You Gaze At The Heavens, With Such Fervour And Might,

Does Anyone Truly Dwell In That Luminous Light?

Why Does This Unease Continue To Grow?

Only One Person Existed In My World, And That's All I Know."

143. MEET ME

" If You Come To Meet Me, The Whole World Will Sway In Joy,

The Very Weather Will Change If You Come To Meet Me,

When You're Not Here, My Only Companions Are My Sorrows,

The World Itself Would Burn With Envy If You Come To Meet Me.

All The Quarrels Of The World And Mundane Conversations Fade Away,

Everything Would Lose Its Importance If You Come To Meet Me. "

144. LOVE'S CURE

" My Heart Is Broken, Yet I Still Breathe,

I Crave Some Potions,

Bitter As They Weave.

You Ask If I'm Well,

Your Concern Is Pure,

I'm Fine Inside, But I Seek Love's Cure."

145. YOUR INDIFFERENCE

" We Were Different In Our Ways Of Living,

Yet Love's Sweet Truth Was Never Given.

Now, How Can I Express The Depths Of My Despair,

When Your Indifference Has Left Me Bare?

In The Realm Of Love, I Find Myself So Small,

Each Glance You Cast Feels Like A Distant Call.

I've Endured The Shadows, The Silent Nights,

Hoping For A Spark, Some Guiding Lights.

Oh, The Longing That Consumes My Heart,

A Dance Of Dreams Where We Played Our Part.

But Now Your Gaze Seems To Wander Away,

Leaving Me Lost, In Silence I Sway.

Yet Still, I Cherish The Moments We Shared,

In Laughter And Whispers, How Deeply We Cared.

Though Your Absence Stings Like A Bitter Breeze,

My Love For You Remains, A Timeless Freeze.

So Here I Stand, With My Heart In My Hand,

A Fragile Soul In This Vast, Lonely Land,

Will You Ever See The Depths Of My Plea,

Or Am I Destined To Love You Silently?

146. GLIMPSE OF YOU

" *A Desire So Deep, It Resides In My Soul,*

Yet Fate Has Woven A Tale That Feels So Whole.

A Glimpse Of You, My Love, Remains Just A Dream,

As I Wander Through Shadows, Lost In This Gleam.

In Every Heartbeat, Your Name Softly Sighs,

In The Silence Of Night, Under The Starry Skies.

I Long For Your Laughter, The Warmth Of Your Gaze,

But The Universe Conspires, Leaving Me In A Haze.

Your Beauty, A Treasure, I Yearn To Behold,

Yet Destiny's Hand Keeps Your Light Untold.

Each Moment Apart Feels Like An Eternity,

As I Chase The Echoes Of What Could Never Be.

But Still, I Hold Onto Hope, With A Heart Full Of Grace,

For Love, Even Unseen, Can Fill Empty Space.

So I Write These Verses, Pouring Out My Plea,

Hoping One Day, My Dove, You'll Come Back To Me."

" There Is A Strange Restlessness That Exists Without You!

I Manage To Live, Yet I Can't Seem To Let Go."

147. GUEST

" I Was A Guest In Your City For Just Two Days,

Now That I'm Leaving, I Can't Even Decide,

Life Feels Like A Fragile Bridge Breaking,

Where I Can Neither Stay Nor Let Time Glide.

In Those Fleeting Moments, Each Heartbeat Whispered,

The Beauty Of Your Laughter, The Warmth Of Your Grace.

I Wished For Eternity, Yet Time Slipped Away,

As If The Universe Conspired To Make Me Stay.

Oh, How I Longed To Linger In Your Embrace,

To Capture The Essence Of Your Every Trace.

But Life Is A River, Flowing Endlessly,

And Here I Stand, Torn Between Memories And Reality.

If Only I Could Pause This Relentless Clock,

To Savor Your Smile, To Feel Love's Sweet Shock.

Yet, As I Turn To Leave, The Ache Is Profound,

In This Bittersweet Parting, My Heart Feels Unbound.

Knows That Every Moment Spent With You,

Is Etched In My Soul, Forever True.

As I Walk Away, I Carry Your Light,

A Love That Transcends The Day And The Night"

148.YOUR PRESENCE

" There Are Many Beautiful Sights To Behold,

But Nothing Compares To Your Presence, Bold.

In This Vast World, Where Wonders Reside,

Mountains And Rivers, With Nature As Guide,

The Sunsets Paint Skies In Hues So Divine,

Yet Your Smile Outshines Them, So Pure, So Fine.

When The Stars Twinkle And The Moon Takes Flight,

Even The Night Pales In Your Radiant Light.

With Every Heartbeat, My Love For You Grows,

In Your Eyes, I See Dreams That Nobody Knows"

" My Eyes Must Have Seen You With So Much Affection And Care,

That No Face Has Looked Beautiful After You. "

149. TOO OLD

" Has My Heart Become Illuminated?

Has Every Bit Of Me Turned Into A Star?

Those Who Bring New Things Into Their Homes,

Have I Become Too Old, Too Familiar?

Those Who Run Away From Their Homes?

Do They Know If Love Has Found A Way?

150. WITHOUT HER

" There Is An Ocean That Resides Within My Arms,

And A Drop That I Cannot Hold Onto,

There Is A Lifetime To Be Lived Without Her,

And A Moment That I Cannot Endure Without Her."

151. DREAMING

" We Will Stay Awake,

We Will Keep Dreaming Of You,

You Will Search Elsewhere,

We Will Bloom Somewhere Else.

Every Season Is A Message Of You!

If You Want, We Will Stay Alive.

When Will You Return, Dear?

We Will Always Call Out Habitually To You.

The Issue In Reaching You Is This;

We Will Remain Haunted By Losing You. "

152. MY LAST LOVE!

" You Are Not Reality; You Are My Desire,

The Treasure Found Only In Dreams That Inspire.

I Live Only Through Your Essence And Light,

If You Ever Tire Of Me, I'd Gladly Take Flight.

With You, Dreams Become Fragrant And Sweet,

A Beauty So Profound, So Elegantly Complete.

You Sit Beside Me, Yet Peace Feels Amiss,

It's As If Parting Shadows Our Bliss.

How Can I Ever Let You Go From My Grasp?

You're The Rhythm Of My Life, The Breath In My Gasp.

Why Do You Look In The Mirror, My Dear?

You're More Beautiful Than Any Reflection Held Near.

This Tale Is Nearing Its Poignant End,

You Are My Last Love, My Heart To Defend.!

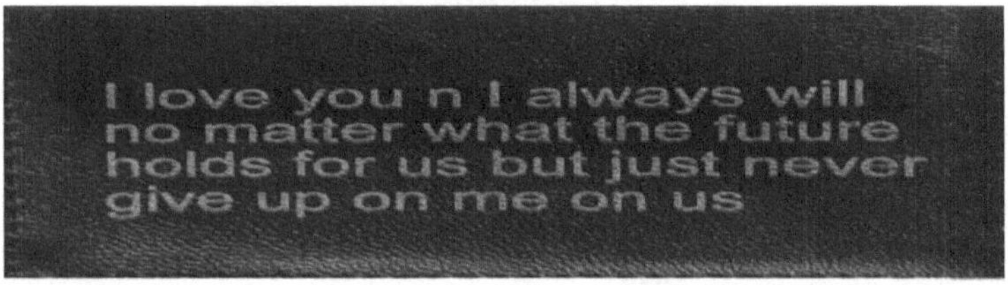

I love you n I always will
no matter what the future
holds for us but just never
give up on me on us

I WILL NEVER GIVE UP ON YOU MY DOVE!

THANK YOU

www.ingramcontent.com/pod-product-compliance
Lightning Source LLC
Chambersburg PA
CBHW051140130726
47988CB00005B/1916